Hengameh Haj Hassan

Face to Face with the Beast

Iranian women in mullahs' prisons

Translated by
Carolyn Beckingham

Face to Face with the Beast
Iranian women in mullahs' prisons

By: Hengameh Haj Hassan
Translated by: Carolyn Beckingham
First Edition: Winter 2013
ISBN: 978-2-9521711-7-5

HOMA Association
for Publication & Communication

انجمن هما

14 -16 Rue Saint Hilaire. B.P.70745 St. Ouen L'Aumone
95004 Cergy-Pontoise Cedex, France
www.homa-association.com
Email: info@homa-association.com

This book is dedicated to Shekar and all the Shekars,
anonymous messengers of freedom
who, faced with the Beast in power in Iran,
the devourer of women and men,
rebelled, resisted it
and defended the human race,
its honour and its liberty.

Preface

When you take up your pen to relate, years later, the events and memories of your imprisonment, you are caught in the crossfire of contradictory feelings and thoughts. The first question that comes to your mind is: Can you? Are you capable of making those astonishing moments and memories live again? Hasn't the veil of time covered them to the point of masking them and making them disappear? Can you retrace, even very schematically, that unimaginable universe? Infallibly, these questions are followed by the usual litanies: *"Now let's get serious! Writing isn't everybody's job. Accredited writers have already written about Khomeini's prisons, they have certainly described those things. What do you want to add? And besides, you were simply a prisoner, you were only imprisoned for three years. And during the interrogation, you weren't beaten and tortured as much as all the rest, because Tahmineh took it all on herself and endured all the consequences. You didn't even taste one thousandth of what many other prisoners endured. So let those who are more capable write about the tragedies and the realities of prison..."* And a thousand and one other remarks, and a thousand and one other doubts of this kind besieged me.

Finally one thought and one feeling prevailed: all I have read and heard about the prisons and the regime of the mullahs –and God knows I've read plenty– only represents one drop in that flood of atrocities. Because apart from the fact that this ocean of suffering and violence cannot be contained within the mind and the pen of one person, the victims of the massacre, the direct targets of that flood of torture and cruelty never came out of prison to tell what happened to them. Those heroic people *"gave their lives without a cry"*. So who is to make their voices heard?

This is why, even if what I write is only the reflection of my three years of incarceration –I have not integrated all the accounts of prison which have reached me– even if what I know only provides a very partial witness account of the infinite cruelty of Khomeini's executioners; even if I know in advance that I can only show one aspect of the resistance of the People's Mojahedin[1], and that at best I shall only have poured one more drop onto the preceding drops, the fact is that this is indispensable. I must therefore put pressure on my mind and heart, in spite of all the suffering that those bitter moments revive in me, to make this drop round out and make it run onto the paper.

I must make them heard, those voices that only wanted freedom, only to live free. I must make it heard, the stifled cry of little Fati who was barely fourteen years old, overflowing with life and the ardent hope of seeing her mother again and who found herself brutally faced with the execution squad. I must answer the question asked by Rouzbeh, who was only four, and all the other Rouzbehs,

---

1. The People's Mojahedin Organisation of Iran (PMOI), a movement of opposition to the dictatorial regime of the Shah and the main opposition to the despotic rule of the mullahs in Iran.

who, every night, as they were about to go to sleep, asked their mother: *"Tell me, what was the matter with Daddy?"*

I must tell what they did to the best men and women of my country in *"the cage"* and *"the coffin"*. I must register, somewhere, at least a scrap of what they did to my gentle Shekar and all the other beloved ones.

Perhaps… perhaps the executioners who still unfortunately rule my country will no longer be able to commit those atrocities so easily. Perhaps, throughout the world, the enemies of freedom who, in the name of religion or any other sacred concept, are determined to devour the human race, will fail in their damned plans.

Perhaps … perhaps the people in love with freedom and human values, the awakened consciences, of whom there are many in the world, will rise and come to support the Iranians and their resistance movement, who only want freedom.

But where do I begin? Where do I plunge into that sea of blood and suffering? After much reflection, I decided that it was necessary to recall, in a few lines or a few pages, the social atmosphere of Iran at that period, by evoking the first years of the anti-monarchist revolution. For even if prison can appear to be an isolated environment, it is in reality an integral part of society; more precisely, it is the continuation of the fight which the people are conducting against a minority which has taken over power. Barbarity and oppression, omnipresent in society, become routine in prison. Resistance, present everywhere in the most varied forms, is concentrated there, and expresses itself fully in the prisoners' heroism.

It seems that prisons, at least Iranian political prisons, are where the torturers' cruelty and bestiality reach a paroxysm. They are one of the poisoned fruits of Khomeini's fundamentalism and retrograde outlook; that is where some people's weaknesses and hollow pretentions show themselves most forcefully. But that is also where the Iranian people's ardent thirst for freedom reaches its summit thanks to the resistance of its bravest children. The mentality and the philosophy of the Iranian resistance are brilliantly illustrated there.

So, although this book essentially contains my personal memories and experience of Khomeini's prisons, I wished first of all to recall the climate of Iranian society at that period.

Part One
Iran in 1981

A student nurse during the revolution

Perhaps, it's not extraordinary for a student nurse to be in symbiosis with the revolution, that is to say wanting liberty and freedom for her people. But at that time, I was a stranger to politics, I was unaware of the nature and the thoughts of the various groups and I didn't know about those who had just taken power and who were ruling us. I was thirsty for knowledge and my mind was innocent of any preconceived ideas. I think that helped me to understand the various political currents and judge their sincerity.

I literally devoured all the publications I could lay hands on. With the relative freedom that existed just after the revolution, everything was accessible. I attended all the meetings and all the speeches. As time went on, the political skein began to unravel. Thus I understood that in spite of the similarity of what they said, the groups were totally different in practice. Little by little, I felt that the Mojahedin, in their thoughts, their ideology and their actions, were distinct from the others. I therefore found them more attractive and more sincere, and their words went so straight to my heart such that I felt as if they were my own words.

At first, I could not understand why the Mojahedin were subjected to such repression; those people, with the greatest selflessness, were seeking only to meet the population's fundamental needs. They wanted neither power, nor any particular post. Why were the mullahs, who were in power and who were Muslims, the sworn enemies of the Mojahedin who were also Muslims? I was not yet mature enough to realise that the root of their conflict derived precisely from two antagonistic visions of Islam. For the former, Islam was a means of gaining power and repressing the people in order to keep the power, and for the latter, Islam was synonymous with freedom, tolerance and the well-being of everyone.

With my friends and colleagues, Shekar Mohammad-Zadeh, Tahmineh Rastegar-Moghadam, Touba Rajabi-Thani, Kobra Alizadeh, Akram Bahador and Ezat, the best and the most agreeable in my academic year, we rapidly opted for the Mojahedin as our only hope for opposing the fundamentalist mullahs. In 1979, we set out on a path from which there was no turning back. We did not yet know, and we could not imagine, the amount of suffering and difficulties that awaited us there. As the poet Hafez said: *"Love seemed easy at first, then the difficulties arose..."*

I should also like to add that as a woman, and in spite of my sympathy with the Mojahedin, one doubt remained in my mind. I questioned myself about their conception of womanhood. I asked myself why Mojahedin women wore a headscarf. At their meetings, I was forever expecting someone to ask me why I wasn't wearing one. I wanted to know if sanctions would be imposed on me because of

that. Would I be looked on differently? Would people behave towards me like the mullahs, who state that I am only
half as good as a man? Nothing like that ever happened.
My last doubts were dispelled during the political actions,
such as the demonstration against Khomeini's and his supporters' order: *"The headscarf or a blow on the head."* I was
bareheaded and I demonstrated beside Mojahedin women
against compulsory veiling, and we were bludgeoned together by hooligans and Khomeini's thugs. When I saw
with what determination they defended women's right to
dress as they please, I was sure of having found what I was
looking for.

In the spring of 1979, I ran into Farideh, a colleague
of mine at the Thousand-Bed Hospital (later the Khomeini
Hospital), who, together with medical students, was distributing Mojahedin tracts. I hastened to join them.

"I want to participate and help you too," I called out.

"Not today, but you can come later," they answered,
laughing.

What did that mean? Why didn't they accept me? Perhaps it was because I wasn't wearing a headscarf like them.

*"I'll follow you all the same, whether you want me to or
not, you can't stop me!"*

"All right, stay there, I'm coming back," said Farideh.

I understood that she had gone to announce the arrival
of a new recruit to their team. They took me with them
and that's how my work began: we distributed posters and
stuck them up, we sold the newspaper and books, we cam-
paigned for candidates at elections. We did it all day and
almost every day, we were confronted by the aggressiveness
of the hooligans who were now called *Hezbollahis*. We often came back with swollen faces. But we were under or-

ders not to answer violence in kind. Our task was peaceful. We needed to reveal the true nature of Khomeini and his regime.

One day, hooligans surrounded a schoolgirl who was selling the newspaper in Hassanabad Square in Tehran. They insulted and hit her, they tried to seize her newspapers and tear them up. The girl resisted and protected the papers with her body. Her slim figure sustained an avalanche of punches and kicks, blows with chains and sticks. She held out until the store owners and residents in the neighbourhood came to her help and got her out, her face bloodied and her clothes in tatters.

The same thing happened to me in Doctor-Fatemi Street and it was the workers in the block across the road who came to my help. They drove the Hezbollahis away and picked up my newspapers which were torn to pieces. They gave them back to me, paid me more money than they were worth and then kindly escorted me home.

I understood thus in practice what I had read in books, I paid with my person. I learned this great lesson: those who have power, mullahs in particular, don't let it go easily. They hang on to it with all their force and will do anything to keep it. But I admit that my notion of "anything" and of "all the crimes" that the mullahs will commit in order to hang on to that power was very naïve in comparison with what I was about to discover in prison.

The compulsory headscarf, means of repressing and humiliating women

When the headscarf became compulsory, there was a riot, especially in my workplace, the hospital. For nurses' uniform, with its pretty white cap and special overall, forms part of their profession's trademark image. Nurses resisted the archaic decision of those in power to modify their dress. It was therefore far from easy for the regime to achieve its aims.

I admit that I wanted to become a nurse from childhood and that it was the dress which first attracted me. In my childish imagination, with that dress and that pretty cap, a nurse looked like an angel with white wings who appeared at the patients' bedside, gliding with a swift, light step, lit with the sweetness of her smile, relieving the patients' pain and tending their wounds with her skilful and attentive hands. Now I saw that fairy tale turn into a nightmare. Most of my friends and colleagues, whose characters I knew, felt more or less the same way. That's why resistance lasted for days and weeks. Little by little, we found ourselves faced with groups of people who threw acid in women's faces and deluged them with obscene insults, making their lives impossible. All so as to make them abandon their social life.

My friends Tahmineh Rastegar-Moghadam, who worked at the Sina Hospital, Shekar Mohammad-Zadeh, who at that time was employed at the Thousand-Bed Hospital, and myself, had been identified as opponents and we were often used as targets. Unlike me, they both wore the headscarf, which they had freely chosen. But that didn't spare them the fundamentalists' anger. So the compulsory headscarf was not only the fruit of the mullahs' backwardness, it was also a means of repressing, first, women, then the whole of society. However, the political climate did not yet allow these acts of violence and injustice to be committed officially. They therefore depended on bands of yobs charged with officiously enforcing repression.

For instance, they had made the porter at the entrance to note the names of all women who came to the hospital without headscarves. Once or twice, the porter stopped me on my arrival and asked me to cover my head. I refused. Then one day, he took me aside and said: *"Madam, they threatened to expell me if I didn't give the names of women without headscarves. But I'd rather starve. I don't want to be in their pay. I beg you, to avoid giving them an excuse, just before you go in, put something on your head and when you're inside, take it off. I have a family, you see, and if they sack me, I won't be able to feed them and I'll make them miserable."* I answered him: *"Write my name, I shan't hold it against you. I know you're obligated to do it. But please understand that I refuse their orders and this insult."* And I was really ready to hold out, even if the price was my life.

During these incidents, Shekar was expelled from the hospital on the odious and trumped-up pretext that she was hanging around the men's dormitory. When the news spread, the whole hospital was indignant, because everyone knew Shekar and knew that they were trying to slander her. A wave of protests broke out, from the doctors to the nurses.

Shekar's mother even came to the hospital to complain: *"I shall force you to tell the truth,"* she shouted. *"Admit you sacked her because she supported the Mojahedin! You gang of cowards, you don't dare say so! You accuse her of your own swinishness! It's an honour for my daughter to have been sacked for supporting the Mojahedin! I shan't let you punish her for what you do yourselves!"*

The repercussions were on such a scale that the mullahs were forced to annul her sacking and take her back.

But they moved her to a different institution because they could not accept their defeat and they also wanted to be obeyed by the use of such methods.

Shekar came to work at Sina with me. In order to give more substantial financial help to the Mojahedin, she was also employed in a private clinic in Tehran: Apadana.

20 June 1981 and its consequences

We had pursued our activities for making the Mojahedin better known until 20 June 1981. It was on that day, as historic as it was bloodstained, that Khomeini's savagery earned an indelible place in history.

On 20 June, I was on duty and I knew that the Mojahedin were organising a peaceful demonstration. Suddenly, during the afternoon, the hospital had filled up with people with bullet wounds and corpses. The corpses were put in the morgue and the wounded divided between the wards and the operating theatre. All of them had been hit by firearms. We had been informed by the other hospitals that the *pasdaran*, the *"Islamic Revolutionary Guards"*, had invaded the hospitals and ruthlessly arrested all the wounded, even those who were already hospitalised. We then decided to take some measures to protect our patients. With some of our colleagues, we immediately sent away the lightly wounded, and hid the more seriously hurt people, including those in a coma, among the other patients. Even the regime's informers couldn't find them. Apart from the body of a schoolboy killed by a bullet right in the forehead, whom the pasdaran took away, we managed to protect them all.

The next day, 21 June, the pasdaran entered the hospital to arrest us because we were known for our support of the Mojahedin. Colleagues who were waiting on the way warned us in time. Everyone knew more or less that if we were arrested, what had happened to the demonstrators would happen to us. In fact, from the evening of 20 June onwards the executions began, including those of students and schoolchildren, even prior to identifying them.

"Crime: caring for the wounded"

Everyone was in shock. Nobody believed what they saw or heard. Shekar was arrested on 21 June at Apadana Hospital. Because of the great number of wounded, she had been working non-stop for twenty-four hours. She was in the middle of nursing them, when they came looking for her to take her to Evin prison. With Tahmineh and other colleagues, we managed to run away and hide.

We couldn't go home again, because they were waiting for us there. The strangest thing was that our crime, as they told our families, was *"having cared for the wounded"*. Now that was our profession and no law in the world can prevent a doctor or a nurse from doing it. It is the first and only duty of a health professional, but, under Khomeini's regime, it was a crime punishable by death.

While I was on the run, I worked discreetly during the day at private clinics, in order to have somewhere to go. At night, when I wasn't on duty, I stayed with friends or relatives.

One evening, when I was on duty at Sajjad (formerly Shahram) Hospital in Doctor-Fatemi Square, armed guards brought in three young people aged 16 or 17, with bullet wounds. They accused them of supporting the Mojahedin. As they had resisted arrest, the pasdaran had fired on them.

We immediately led them to the operating theatre. The armed pasdaran came in with us, to stay near the wounded. When the doctor protested and asked them to leave, they not only refused, but they aimed and threatened to fire on him. As soon as the operation was over, before the patients had even regained consciousness, they transferred the first two of the wounded to Evin prison.

After they left, the theatre staff and all those affected by this affair decided to stop working. I think that at that moment we all felt the same way. We had reached this paradox: it was against all that we had been taught, but we asked ourselves if it would have been better not to save them. What use had our care been? Hadn't we, by doing this, sent them to torture? Doubt gnawed me and I felt powerless. Never had I felt so useless and so lost.

And there, unconscious, alone and defenceless, lay the young wounded man that I was trying at all costs to save. He was in the hands of those barbarians and he would soon be one of the executed. And the authorities were not even taking the trouble to ask their names.

An adolescent at death's door

Given that the third man had been hit by a bullet in the face, he was in a serious condition and had been given resuscitation. A few of the staff were watching his weakened and bloodstained body. After the pasdaran left with the other two wounded, we nurses swore, without planning or consulting one another, not to let them have that one.

On the pretext of giving him auscultation, I went to his bedside and asked another colleague to distract the attention of the staff so that I could say a few words to him. While caring for him and taking his blood pressure, I murmured: *"If you can hear me, listen! I am your friend, I am in favour of the Mojahedin. I am telling you the symptoms of a convulsion after a cranial trauma: arm and leg movements, snoring… When I tell you, show me those symptoms."* After a few minutes, he did it. Therefore he was conscious.

He was very young, like my little brother, who was at school. My dear brother, he was clever, intelligent, but noisy and talkative. He played football in the neighbourhood, he did silly things and annoyed my little sister. Besides, my mother had to watch him continually so as to prevent him being a nuisance to the neighbours. But everyone loved that turbulent, nice young boy. Sometimes he helped the local residents, bought bread for them, jumped over the wall to open the door when they left the key inside by mistake … Often he brought home a wounded cat or bird that he looked after, hiding it from my mother. He asked me to help him and not let them die.

And now a boy of his age was there, exactly like him. All he had done was read a newspaper or participated in some school sporting activity in the company of young supporters of the Mojahedin. Perhaps he had spoken of the organisation and defended it. A bullet had hit him and he was fighting death in a hospital bed.

During the two or three days that he remained alive, we tried to get him out of there. But armed pasdaran sat beside him night and day, in the intensive care unit. And his wound was too severe for anything to be done. Yet an opportunity did present itself. The pasdar[1] , who was keeping watch, had left for a few minutes to go to the lavatories. The nurse on duty, who was waiting for that moment, rushed to the boy's bedside, asked him to trust her and give her his name and address. Hearing the nurse's voice, he tried to open his eyes. He only managed to open one, the other being closed by a haematoma. As he could not speak, he traced his parents' name and telephone number with one finger on the bed.

He was called Hossein. He had light brown eyes, shining and innocent, and although he was lying between life and death, the look in them was full of hope. A vigilant and determined look that evinced a will to succeed at any cost. A faint smile touched his swollen and bruised lips, to thank us. We felt that he wanted to see the faces of the men and women who were caring for him.

We were able to let his parents know. We asked them to come and see him from a long way off and not show they knew him, because Khomeini's torturers were watching like vultures for the slightest indication that might enable them to identify him. That was how they could, as they said themselves, identify the others and torture them in turn, to satisfy their hatred.

His mother came to visit her lonely and wounded son. But she had to stay by another patient in a coma. She shed torrents of tears, like rain in the North of Iran, in silence. She was seeing her son suffer and die a few steps away from her. She was seeing the gaping jaws of death swallowing her child. And she could not come near him, nor lighten his suffering with a simple caress.

---

1. Singular form of pasdaran, in Persian.

At that moment, probably, she wished with all her heart just to touch her little one's head, sponge his feverish face and kiss his forehead to feel the warmth of life in him. Perhaps she was thinking of the lullabies she used to sing to him or the silly things he had done. Perhaps she was thinking of the future she had built for that intelligent, brave boy. Sometimes her lips trembled as if she was speaking, perhaps she was praying. At all events, she was begging imperturbably with the whole of her being. She went on watching her son from afar, and crying. She was not allowed to approach him. We watched them both, trying to hold back our tears, because Khomeini's wild beasts were there.

Hossein, who was in a coma at death's door, never knew that his mother had come to see him. After three days, the last glimmers of life left him.

Shekar's story

After Shekar's arrest, we knew no peace. Her mother was desperately looking everywhere for her, but none of the forces of repression gave any news of her. Every day the radio and television announced the names of tens and hundreds of people executed. The newspapers published photographs of some of them, asking their parents to go and identify them in order to retrieve their bodies. The mullahs condemned people to death without even knowing their names. They knew very well what they were doing: they wanted to terrify the population.

Shekar was one of those whose name appeared nowhere. Only her colleagues at the hospital had seen her taken away by force because she resisted the armed pasdaran. They had torn off her headscarf and seized her by the hair. Under the horrified and weeping eyes of the patients and her colleagues, they had thrown her violently into their vehicle and driven off.

Since then, the pasdaran and the other cogs in the regime denied her arrest. Her mother was searching in vain for traces of her in front of prison doors, in cemeteries and in the pages of the newspapers.

After about a month, we learned that Shekar had been "interrogated", that is to say tortured at Evin prison. As they had nothing against her, they had severely tortured her in order to obtain confessions that would have allowed them to justify her arrest and allowed them to condemn her to death. But Shekar, that benevolent nurse with a deep sense of responsibility, resisted them. *"By nursing the wounded, I was only doing my duty and I'll do it again,"* she flung at them. *"You're the ones who should be judged. Why did you kill or wound them? If one wants to be fair, you should be condemned to death so that people can be rid of you. You judge us when it's you who are the assassins!"* It was a pasdar who told her mother about that, in order to prove her guilt.

Although she had never committed any crime, Shekar was condemned to fifteen years of prison on the pretext that she had helped wounded Mojahedin. Time has proved that the mullahs did not even respect that unjust sentence.

When I was imprisoned later, Shekar told me that during the interrogation period, she and the other prisoners hadn't had any means of taking a shower. They had suffered from hunger because they were given nothing to eat except a spoonful of beans or a few spoonful of rice for eight people. Shekar said that the beans were shared out: a meal was limited to four beans per person. By these forms of pressure, which I suffered later, they wanted to break the girls' resistance. Shekar and many others did indeed fall ill and were never able to recover. Shekar suffered several digestive haemorrhages. She would vomit everything she ate and became extremely weak.

From 20 June to 10 November 1981, the date on which I was arrested, I lived in hiding. I could no longer go home. Fortunately, thanks to my profession and with the help of friends, I was able to take on employment in private clinics. I worked day and night, in order to not have to go home or to my relatives. Especially as the pasdaran had raided our home and taken away my little sister in my stead. After months of trying, my father had managed to get her out of their claws. However it might be, when I wasn't at the hospital, I walked the streets for hours on the pretext of going round the shops, because there was no safe place.

We were organised in teams and went on with our work. Tahmineh, Ezat and I were in the same group. We secretly helped the organisation. We denounced Khomeini and the mullahs and had whip-rounds among the people.

The more killing our enemies did, the more they proved to us that we had made the right choice and reinforced our conviction that they must be conquered. The more people they executed, the more our determination increased and we felt the weight of the responsibility for every death and every prisoner on our shoulders. Those were the foundations of the struggle we had chosen.

Five months went by during which many colleagues, friends and comrades were arrested. Akram Bahador, Touba Rajabi-Thani, Doctors Sadegh Aghamsheh, Doroudian, Fahimeh Mir Ahmadi, Nahid Tahsili, and every day we heard of more executions and imprisonments. Akram Bahador, the only one who was still in prison, was executed during the massacre of political prisoners in 1988[2]. Doctor Fahimeh Mir Ahmadi, an intern at Sina Hospital, was murdered at home along with her husband when she was pregnant. The pasdaran committed these murders on the pretext of having seized one of the organisation's bases.

Fahimeh had been my superior in the hierarchy for a time. The last time I saw her in the street, she had told me of the execution of Touba Rajabi-Thani, and of Doctors Aghamsheh and Nahid Tahsili.

Touba, her brother and sister's only hope

Touba was a girl who had grown up alone. She had lost both her parents in an earthquake. She had a younger brother and a younger sister, who lived with close relatives. She herself lived with a relative in the North of Iran and, after passing her examination, she had come to Tehran to study nursing. Touba was extremely studious and spoke very little.

One day when she was sitting on a bench by the water basin reading a letter, I came up to her from behind and, to tease her, covered her eyes with my hands. Suddenly, I felt my fingers grow wet and realised that she was crying. I was sorry for my joke. I felt uneasy. I sat down opposite her and while she tried to smile at me through her tears, she held out her letter to me.

---

2. Khomeini proclaimed a fatwa for the massacre of the Mojahedin prisoners. "Death committees" were constituted in all the prisons and in the space of three months 30,000 prisoners were executed after a show trial. Khomeini wanted to rid himself in this way of the Resistance after the ceasefire with Iraq.

It was her little sister who was writing to her: *"To have the right to go to school, I have to do their cleaning and in the evening I have to mind their child. I also watch over my little brother. My dear Touba, I am very tired. In the morning, I'm late for school and I fall asleep in class. Luckily the teacher knows what situation we're in and says nothing."* She went on: *"We're both just waiting for you to finish your studies, rent a room and take us in. I beg you, please hurry up, finish your studies and take us with you."*

Touba was never able to take a lodging for her little family and make their dreams come true. Khomeini's executioners killed her. Because she had chosen the path of the Mojahedin in order to make the dreams of all children without families and relatives, come true. She had been betrayed by the hospital Hezbollahis, then arrested and executed. Did her little sister know it? Or did she still hope that she would rent a maid's room in Tehran where she could bring them?

These thoughts flooded me and tears came to my eyes. Fahimeh, who also found it hard to control herself, whispered to me: *"These lives are the price of freedom and we must be ready too."*

Doctor Fahimeh Mir Ahmadi, who was the indefatigable intern dealing with Sina Hospital's emergencies, was executed very quickly with her child who never came into the world. I shall never forget those friends, those sisters.

They stood up to Khomeini's horror and told him: *"No!"* And by their blood, they kept alight the torch of respect for the people who in their eyes symbolised the Mojahedin and their humanist values.

I cannot envisage the destiny of Iranian society without them and without their sacrifices.

Arrest in the street

One autumn day, 8 November 1981, after having gone with Tahmineh to Shekar's parents to hear if there was any news of her, I got out of a taxi in Kennedy Square. As the street was deserted and I didn't feel safe, I went into a fabric dealer's store. There were two women in the shop, one of them with a child in her arms. Suddenly, a vehicle stopped in front of the shop and two armed men got out. They came into the shop shouting: *"Go on! Get into the car!"* Both women started to cry and the child to howl. I tried to see if I could escape, but it was impossible. There were two guards at the shop door. So I was arrested. From the first few moments, I thought I had been identified. But I noticed that they were going around the streets and questioning everybody aged from 15 to 30. As they said themselves, they arrested the suspects first and looked for the crimes afterwards.

In the car, the women were crying. I wasn't crying, but I wanted to flee; they handcuffed me. *"We're going to take you away so that you're dealt with at once,"* said a pasdar, turning around. *"You're going to understand what Massoud[3] has done to you."*

I replied: *"Whose lackey are you, dog? What's this hatred of Massoud that makes you want to let off steam on me? And who do you think you are, saying his name with your filthy mouth?"*

He covered me with curses, lifting his fist to hit me.

I said: *"Luckily you're not clever enough to understand what you're saying in front of ordinary people whom you'll have to let go. You show yourselves as you are, disgusting, and those people will never need any further explanations."*

---

3. Allusion to Massoud Rajavi, leader of the Resistance.

"*Shut her up, both of you!*" shouted a pasdar who seemed to be the boss.

"*Shut up yourselves, both of you!*" I retorted … And said no more.

"*You'll get your answer! In your big mouth!*"

They took us to a *committee*[4] near Kennedy Square and threw us into an empty, dark room in the basement. I don't know how many hours went by. It was dark. Little by little, I felt the fear of solitude, a strange fear, no doubt that of death. I wondered how one dies. I had seen patients die, but as to being subjected to the process myself, I had never thought about it. But I thought about it there.

The door of the room opened and the pasdaran came to fetch us and put us into another vehicle. The women went on crying, begging and endlessly giving their addresses. Obviously they had made enquiries, because they released them.

I saw our street in the distance, when we were passing in front of *Parkway*. I asked myself what my mother was doing and thinking about at that moment. She was certainly a hundred miles from imagining what was happening to me. But it wouldn't be long before she noticed my absence and she would do the rounds of the prisons and cemeteries. If only I had been able to tell her where I was going!

When I found myself alone, they blindfolded me and beat me black and blue, and then stretched me out on the floor of the car, hitting and cursing me. And they drove off towards Evin – as I understood later.

---

4. Neighbourhood centres of repression. They were composed of armed hooligans who later joined, and then dominated, the forces of law and order and the police.

I was eaten up with anxiety. I asked myself where they were taking me and what they were going to do with me. If they asked me about Tahmineh, what should I answer? If they asked me where I had been during that period, if they wanted addresses, what should I say? A multitude of questions were thrown at me and it was impossible for me to concentrate under the rain of blows and curses. We had finally arrived and I was taken to the second section of Evin prison. They made me sit on a chair, facing the wall, in the corner of an empty room. I asked myself where I was and what they wanted to do to me. I was worried about Tahmineh. Would she learn about my arrest? What had happened to her? Because she was in the street too, and with their methods she ran a high risk of being arrested. I so wished I could have told her not to go out. But what could I do while in the hands of those savages?

Part Two

Evin Prison

First Interrogation

All the time I was sitting down, I heard strange, stifled cries coming from each corner, and a regular noise like that of blows landing on a carpet during the spring cleaning for the new year[1]. My mother used to hang up the carpet and beat it with all her force to make the dust come out. But however hard I tried, I couldn't understand where that noise came from.

My heart wouldn't stay in place. I felt it beating right up in my throat. Those noises ... What is it? What are they trying to do? I had prepared myself for being executed, especially as they had done some investigation and knew I was a nurse at Sina Hospital. But what if they didn't want to execute me? They would certainly torture me. I didn't know what torture was, but I was terrified of it.

During the investigation, they had found in my bag a list of people who made donations to us and a manuscript tract from the Mojahedin. Fortunately, I had only written down the people's first names and they couldn't learn anything from it. Suddenly I decided to resist right to the end,

---

1. The Iranian New Year, *Nowrouz*, is on 21 March, the Spring Equinox.

whatever the cost. A man came and sat down in front of me. He brought his face so close to mine that I could smell his breath, foetid and disgusting.

With blindfolded eyes, I pulled my head back and asked: *"What do you want?"*

"Listen," he said calmly, *"we know all about it. No use giving yourself and us a headache. You'd better tell us everything and get it over. You're a nice girl and we know it, okay? I'm going to try and help you."*

That imbecile thought he was taking me in by saying that; he took me for a simpleton.

"Sir, how am I supposed to tell you what you know and since you know it, what do you expect me to tell you?"

I was trying to concentrate and not talk too much, I was trying to use ordinary words, like his, so as not to seem too political. I was hoping to give this image of myself in order to gain time, so that Tahmineh and the others would learn about my arrest and avoid the places I frequented.

"Do you know Shahnaz?" the man asked me.

I knew her. For a few months she had been our team leader. She worked at the National Bank of Tehran's hospital. She had been arrested two months earlier, with Firouzeh.

"No, I don't know anyone of that name!"

"But she knows you!"

"Lots of people know me. It's possible that she's seen me somewhere, but I haven't any colleague who's called that."

"Right, just you wait!"

He came back a few minutes later.

"When I tell you to, take your blindfold off and look straight in front of you, not in any other direction."

He placed himself behind me. He didn't want to be identified. During the interrogations, I learned that the questioners were terrified of being recognised. When we passed them, they always wore white cowls with two holes, like members of the Ku Klux Klan. Even when we were blindfolded, they didn't take off their cowls.

I pulled off my blindfold. Shahnaz was in front of me, wearing a black chador. Her expression was cold and life-less. I tried to keep my self-control.

"Ah! It's you, Shahnaz! What are you doing here?" I asked her in the most ordinary way I could, giving her a wink.

"No, Hengameh, I've told them everything. It's no use making signs at me."

I felt as if I had just had a great blow on the head with a bludgeon. I realised that she had given in. It was very painful, as I wasn't prepared for such a thing, especially in front of the enemy! It was as if I had been plunged into boiling water. For a few seconds, I felt I was burning from head to foot, I was dizzy and my mouth dried up. And then I recovered myself, I tried to regain my self-control and think. I tried to remember what she knew about me, I ran rapidly over the information in my head. No, she didn't know anything. She hadn't had any of my news for a year and I hadn't seen her. So she was lying to make me speak.

"I don't give a damn what you know or what you said, I don't know anything. I've nothing to say to the people who killed my friends."

I spoke like that on purpose to make it seem like a personal grudge. She tried again to make me speak. She named the people who had been arrested, those who were in prison. She wanted to gain my confidence and make me weaken.

"It's nothing to do with me if they're there," I answered.
"Tahmineh's there too," she added.

It was as if my heart collapsed. How did they know about Tahmineh? And then it came to me that because I worked in the same hospital as Tahmineh, they wanted me to give them some clues. I told them that I hadn't seen her for months and didn't know where she was.

The first torture

When the interrogator saw that it wasn't doing any good, he led Shahnaz away and laid me face down on the bed of torture. He chained my hands to the top of the bed and my feet to the bottom end, so tightly that, in spite of all my efforts, I couldn't move them. A filthy brute of a pasdar sat down on me and they threw a blanket over my face. That moment that I had thought about for a long time, and for which I was awaiting, was about to come. I was still a prey to questions and doubts when suddenly something very hard hit the soles of my feet. In a flash, a powerful wave, terrifyingly painful, ran over all the nerves of my body like an electric current, shaking me with spasms. At that moment I understood what it was that sounded like a hanging carpet being beaten. More blows followed, I don't remember how many. I howled with pain. Then they untied me. I felt exhausted, worn out, as if I had been digging the ground for hours.

"I don't want to punish you," the interrogator said to me, *"so long as you talk about yourself."* They had, as they called it, Islamicised the word for torture by calling it *"punishment"*. They wanted to make me talk by using the carrot and the stick approach. I had lost all sense of time, it was

night but I no longer knew what time it was. He made me sit down again. *"When I tell you to,"* he said, *"take your blindfold off, but don't say a word. You mustn't be heard."*

After a few seconds, he tapped me on the head with a pencil and said in a low voice: *"Take off your blindfold!"* I took it off and all of a sudden I saw Tahmineh in front of me, standing up with a black blindfold over her eyes. She was wearing her usual outfit, a suit with brown and cream checks. They had arrested her. It was as if the world was collapsing, there were shooting pains in my temples. It had made me forget the pain of the whip, but fatigue overwhelmed me, as if I hadn't slept for a century.

How had they arrested her? How had they known that she and I were close? *"Put your blindfold on!"* ordered the interrogator, and they led her away. In fact Tahmineh didn't know I was there and that she was in front of me. What was I to do now? If they asked her questions and her answers were different from mine, we would both be tortured. My God, if only I could speak to her!

I don't know why the inspector didn't go on with his interrogation that evening. That helped me a lot. They took me into a room where many women were sitting on the ground and others lying down. Some had their feet bandaged. Blood had seeped through their rough bandages and then dried. It was clear that the wounds hadn't been dressed for several days. The smell of blood and sweat saturated the air. As soon as we came in, women with bandaged eyes moaned: *"When are you going to change our dressings!"* Their guards, female pasdaran, gave vague answers. Two of them pulled off my blindfold and began a body search at the door. *"What's happened to their feet?"* I asked. I thought that they had been fired on when they were arrested. I could not imagine that those monsters had torn their feet to shreds by beating them with cables. *"You'll soon know,"* said a female pasdar with a hateful laugh, looking me straight in the eye. Her icy look showed hate and cruelty. As if she had no heart. Lord, how could Khomeini denature people so much?

This room was in fact the ante-room to the torture chamber. Being in the room was already a terrifying psychological torture, even harder to bear than the physical torture. I sat down in a corner. I was shocked and anxious. I managed to look at people from underneath my blindfold. We heard the door open. Two female guards were dragging a woman whose head fell onto her shoulders. Like two black crows or rather, two bin liners, they threw the woman onto the others, in the middle of the room, and then went away again.

The newcomer gave a cry of pain before she collapsed. The others moved away with difficulty and made room for her. By chance, her head was on my side and I was able to see her. She started to moan and vomit. I tried to draw near her. On the pretext of stretching out my legs, I slid towards her. I was afraid that pasdaran women were in the room. I gently stroked her head. *"What happened to you?"* I asked her. Then she turned her head towards me and I recognised her. It was Mahnaz, a student with whom we used to go to the mountains. I had often seen her at the association of student supporters of the Mojahedin.

"Mahnaz, my darling, is it you? It's me, Hengameh! But what happened to you? But what have they done to you?"

"They shredded my feet with cables. I don't think my kidneys are still working. I've urinated blood and I think my nausea and vomiting come from that."

Strangely, it was she who began to boost my confidence. *"Hengameh,"* she whispered in a trembling voice, *"I'm sure it's all over for me. I shall be condemned to death. But you, you must be strong and go on. Tell the others!"* I stroked her head, crying, and then all of a sudden I lost patience: *"She's dying! Call someone to bring her a tranquilliser."* When the guards arrived, she was vomiting incessantly, she was exhausted. I asked them for a tranquilliser. They gave her an injection and she fell asleep.

I was still in the same room when the two pasdaran women came in, bringing another prisoner. They passed in front of me and I recognised her clothes from under the blindfold. Tahmineh! It was she! My heart leapt into my mouth. I followed them to find out what part of the room they were taking her to. I asked myself if they had done it on purpose, to see if I would get in touch with her, or whether it had escaped them because they were so rushed. When the pasdaran left, I told myself that, at all events, this might be my only chance. I slid along, stretched out, in order to get close to her. I put my head near her legs. She was sitting down.

"Tahmineh! Tahmineh!"

She lifted her head so as to look from underneath her blindfold.

"Is it you, Hengameh?" she asked calmly.

I told her everything, at the speed of light: my arrest, what they knew about me, Shahnaz's about-turn, that I had said nothing about her or the others, that they knew nothing, that all they knew came from Shahnaz.

I also told her: *"They brought you in front of me, you were blindfolded. How do they know we know each other?"*

"They decoded the list of your first names that I had noted down. But there are no surnames. So don't let yourself be had, I shan't say anything. They only found out because I had your first name on me. But I told them that you were only a hospital colleague and that I sometimes gave you tracts and that everything you had came from me and you weren't active in any other way."

In fact, Tahmineh had took the blame and sacrificed herself to protect the supporters and all those who helped the organisation. And she had passed off even me, the member of her team, as someone anodyne. She had protected everyone she knew. She had been arrested about an hour after me, in the same way, at random.

Last meeting with Tahmineh

One morning, a pasdar came to look for three prisoners: Tahmineh, another woman and me. We were blindfolded and in order to make us move, the pasdar had a wooden stick whose end he gave to the first prisoner. Then Tahmineh put a hand on her shoulder and I put mine on Tahmineh's. And so we went off in Indian file. He was transferring us from section number 2 to unit 209.

I found out later that unit 209 belonged to the pasdaran, and as we had been arrested by them, we were being brought there. Besides, those who are arrested by the "committees" are interrogated in what they call the Evin annexes. There was no fundamental difference, but it reflected the rivalry and conflicts between their groups. The pasdaran claimed to be better educated; some of them were students. They said they were better at torturing and interrogating. They tried to obtain information, while the members of the "committee" mutilated and killed prisoners straight away. As to the pasdaran, they tortured people in stages. They were helped by the torturers of the Savak (the Shah's secret police) and profited from their experience in order to make the prisoners talk. In fact, Khomeini had succeeded in transforming those students into monsters.

My hand was resting on Tahmineh's shoulder and we were going forward. Something inside me was telling me it was the last time I should touch her and it was causing me anguish. Spontaneously, I gently pressed her shoulder. I think she understood and she put her hand on mine to comfort me. It was our last meeting.

We reached unit 209. They separated us. They led me into a room where they left me alone. All the papers and the evidence they had against me were on a table in front of me. I could see it all from under my blindfold, but I couldn't do anything. I thought they were watching me. Cautiously, little by little, I raised my blindfold and looked all round me. There was no one there. Apparently, they thought we could do nothing and they were right.

I examined the papers. I wanted to take away the one which showed the names of several people, but that was just the one that wasn't there. I had never been interrogated on that subject. I thought they must have lost it on the first night when they used it to threaten me. Perhaps there was someone among them who destroyed that sort of document, because when I was transferred to the general unit, I learned that the critical documents of other prisoners' records had also disappeared.

After a moment, a masked inspector arrived and started his interrogation. I repeated the same thing. Later on, I was interrogated two or three more times. They asked the same questions, in different ways. They thought they could corner me with that idiotic game. I was always reviewing my statements, so as not to forget them.

The most important point was that Tahmineh had taken on herself everything that could be judged as incriminating. That was how she had saved us and that's why she was executed. During my interrogation, they treated me like a commonplace person, convinced that I had fled the hospital for fear of being arrested.

Unit 209 comprised several corridors flanked with individual cells. They shut me into one of them. The pasdaran, who were pushing the prisoners into their cells with little wooden sticks, wanted it to be thought that they avoided touching women in order to respect religious principles. In fact, there was no limit to their offences and outrages. They raped girls before they executed them. I witnessed scenes of sexual humiliation and violation intended to break the prisoners down.

The cell

I went into the cell, a space of two metres wide by two and a half metres long. There were five prisoners there already. In others words, six people in a space meant for one, with a basin and a metal WC bowl: a lack of privacy that was hard to bear. The other problem about this crowding was sleep. There wasn't room enough to stretch out.

Among my companions was Maliheh, a senior-year medical student. I had seen her with the students and medical staff who supported the Mojahedin. I knew her, but according to prison custom, we didn't show any acquaintance until we knew more. She had been atrociously tortured and had been laid full length in the cell. There was also Mehranguiz, arrested in the street because she was judged to be a suspect person. She was in her last month of pregnancy and the conditions of life in the cell were very hard for her. We did our best to help her. There were also two young supporters of the Toudeh[2] and Aksariat[3] political parties, whose names I have forgotten. They had been picked up by mistake and were doing everything to be released. Finally there was a woman of thirty-five who came from North Iran and was called Mother Tal'at. She had been arrested because of her contact with Mojahedin supporters whom she was accused of having helped.

The situation in the cell was a disaster. We had spread out an army blanket on the ground. During the day, one or two other dirty blankets were scattered on the freezing ground, but we picked them up at night to share them as our top cover.

We had no visitors, and in fact, since we had been picked up in the street, the only clothes we had were those that we were wearing: clothes that were dirty and torn because of torture and bleeding wounds. We couldn't wash anything. According to the prison rules, the prisoners in one cell were taken together once a week to another cell which was used as a shower. We had just half an hour for all six of us to wash, clean our clothes and help whoever needed it due to her wounds and torture. She was therefore our priority. We also had to take turns to watch the spy-hole in the door so as to stop the pasdaran from peering viciously inside.

---

2. Toudeh: the Iranian communist party.

3. Aksariat: "Majority Fedayin", one of the branches of the People's Fedayin who are also a Marxist political opposition group. The Toudeh and their allies, the Aksariat, collaborated fully with Khomeini's regime before being persecuted in their turn.

As we had no spare linen, this washing caused problems. Either we washed our clothes and went back to the cell almost naked, hidden under a coat, or we put our wet linen back on and let it dry once we were back in the cell. Sometimes, we left the linen to dry where it was.

In prison, masks fall off

Mehranguiz was a civil servant. She had been arrested in the street and had been waiting for weeks without knowing what was in store for her. Her family had also been left with no news. She often cried. She was troubled when she saw that each of her cellmates was preparing herself for torture or execution. She cursed the leaders of the regime and kept repeating: *"I could never have imagined that the mullahs could do this."* The two Aksariat and Toudeh girls were frantically trying to attract Mehranguiz onto their side.

They therefore put on airs and uttered fine phrases. We didn't interfere, because the situation was so obvious that anyone could see how it really was. One of them said it was necessary to *"have ideological discussions."* As we were suspicious, we retorted: *"It's not the right moment. We've other things to think about."* They assured Mehranguiz that they would stay faithful to their principles and that the Mojahedin wouldn't want to discuss anything with them for fear of running out of arguments.

One day, a pasdar came into the cell with the order to liberate them.

"Have you changed your minds and will you become Muslims?" he asked them.

"Yes!" they hastened to answer.

"And do you pray as well?"

"Yes!" they cried out without the slightest reservation, crying and begging to be freed as soon as possible.

Their attitude toward that imbecile pasdar disgusted us. But it had a certain piquancy when we reflected that a few minutes earlier they had been giving us lessons in how to resist. When their order of liberation had already been signed and they could have left without such excessive begging and pleading, it was pitiable to watch them humiliating themselves like that and transforming themselves into fervent Muslims. Poor Mehranguiz couldn't believe her eyes. *"Don't be surprised,"* I told her, *"the fancy words that they were just uttering meant nothing in practice other than what you just saw. It's under duress that a movement is really tested."*

The communal toothbrush

In our cells, we suffered from a miserable state of hygiene and nutrition. We hadn't been able to brush our teeth for months, and we had no visits because our families didn't even know if we were still alive. The poor people went every day, like Shekar's mother, from prison to prison and cemetery to cemetery.

One of us, during an interrogation, had found an old toothbrush and brought it back. We washed it carefully and, one after the other, we brushed our teeth. Mehranguiz found it very hard to bear, and she wasn't wrong.

The situation was particularly deplorable for Mehranguiz who was reaching the end of her pregnancy and who had no fruit or healthy food. Every day the guards distributed a meal which was not so edible, accompanied by badly cooked industrial bread. The situation was becoming quite unbearable, both for Mehranguiz and the other women, and we didn't know what to do. We had asked for milk for the invalids and our pregnant companion, but we had been given nothing but insults in return. We were continually fighting hunger. Lajevardi[4] plainly admitted it: *"Give the State's budget to a handful of Mojahedin?! Why waste money when they won't stay alive for more than a few days?"*

One evening, Mehranguiz was attacked by violent pains. She was transferred to a hospital outside the prison. We all thought that she was certainly about to give birth and that this would lead to a review of her sentence. How surprised we were when she came back three days later, without having given birth!

"They took me to the hospital," Mehranguiz told us, *"and as soon as the nurses and the staff learned that I had come from prison, they took care of me without the keepers noticing it. I managed to let my family know and tell them where to come for news of me."* She was very happy. The best of it was, she had brought some toothpaste and a little fruit which the hospital staff had given her. That evening, after two or three months, we celebrated by eating oranges, then we brushed our teeth with toothpaste. Mehranguiz was freed a few days later. When she left us, she told us she would never forget us and would do all she could for us. Her liberation filled us with joy.

Maliheh

They had arrested Maliheh in the street. She told us how they had tortured and interrogated her, and how her situation had become intolerable. She had then decided to kill

---

4. Assadollah Lajevardi, boss of Evin Prison, nicknamed "the Butcher", later became the director of the organisation running the country's prisons.

herself: *"When the keeper left the room, I rushed to the window and jumped. But when I reached the bottom, I realised that, unfortunately, I hadn't hurt myself badly. So I pretended I'd fainted."*

The guards hadn't discovered her pretence, because Maliheh was a medical student and knew how to give a perfect imitation of a coma. In spite of the slaps and violent blows the doctor gave her to wake her up, she had shown no reaction. She told me later.

"When I had been given intravenous injection and I was alone, a pasdar came in. He was dirty and repulsive. He wanted to take advantage of the situation to rape me because he thought I had fainted. I couldn't defend myself because I was supposed to be unconscious. That turd came up to me. Then I started miming convulsions and letting bizarre noises come out of my mouth. That frightened him and he left me in peace."

Once she found herself alone, Maliheh tore out her intravenous drip and tried again to kill herself. But she wounded herself again. In spite of her condition, the pasdaran took her straight into the torture chamber and tore her feet to shreds by striking them with cables.

Maliheh was very ill and weakened. She had injured one of her lungs during her suicide attempts, her feet were lacerated by torture, and she had kidney problems. We were the helpless witnesses of the suffering that gave her no rest.

Mother Tal'at

Another woman in our cell was "Mother Tal'at". She was about 35 years old. We gave her that nickname because we were all under 25, and she was also the mother of several small children. She had been arrested with a group of Mojahedin supporters and had been accused of helping them.

Unaffected and clever, Mother Tal'at always managed to make the pasdaran look ridiculous, and when she told us stories, she made us burst out laughing.

The pasdaran torturers thought they were more advanced than the other torturers and, as they said, they interrogated in a scientific manner. Like the Shah's Savak, they acted with as much "respect" as possible for the law. In consequence, so that the interrogation and torture of people who merely happened to be standing around in the street shouldn't have any unfavourable influence on public opinion after their release from prison, instead of torture, they called it "punishment".

Usually, the number of lashes to be given was specified in a sentence read a few moments before being executed by an ersatz judge who was present in the torture chamber. The pasdaran competed in saying again and again that Khomeini said one must not give one lash too many or too few! But it was only words. Because if a prisoner refused to speak or to comply with the guards' demands, the religious judge, who was a torturer himself, inflicted a harder punishment with more lashes. It must be said that they were permitted to do as they pleased, with the support of a famous fatwa of Khomeini's, read on television by the mullah Guilani, President of the Courts of the Islamic Revolution: "the Imam" (Khomeini) had given the torturers a free hand in order to extract confessions from the prisoners.

Mother Tal'at said that one day they had taken her to be questioned and because she didn't give satisfactory answers, her torturer had tied her to the torture table to whip her. He had raised his hands to heaven, saying: *"God! Be my witness that I do not want to whip this woman, but as she does not speak, she obligates me to do it. I am innocent!"*

She was blindfolded, but she raised her hands to heaven saying: *"Lord, you have heard the voice of this unjust man. Hear too my sick woman's voice. Although I tell him I know nothing, he does not believe me and wants to force me with a whip to confess to what I have not done. Lord, be my witness that he is going to strike an innocent woman. Do the same to him!"* Immediately, the torturer started to attack Mother Tal'at with curses and a rain of blows.

On her return, Mother Tal'at told us of her victory, laughing. Every time she came back from an interrogation, she reached fresh conclusions and gave us the benefit of her experience. It was the fruit of her vigilance and her sense of responsibility for conquering the enemy. She said to us: *"Be on your guard, they don't know anything, but those monkeys pretend to know, to frighten us, or to make us believe that they are informed about us. So don't tell them anything, don't let them lead you on. The people who can fool the Mojahedin aren't born yet!"*

When the pasdaran had attacked her house, Mother Tal'at was recovering at home from a surgical operation. They had torn her from her bed under the eyes of her husband and children. Mother Tal'at was a supporter of the Mojahedin. She had been under torture in unit 209 of Evin for about a month. They wanted her to betray other mothers. Not only did she not do it, but, with her formidable vigilance, she managed to make her situation seem ordinary and convince them that she wasn't taking part in any activity. She was freed after a few weeks.

When she left, we gave her the information about our families so that she could let them know, and that's what she did.

In prison the only times when she seemed preoccupied and worried were those when she thought about her fourteen-year-old daughter, Fatemeh. *"The evening when they attacked the house,"* she told us, *"she wasn't there. I'm afraid those wretches may have arrested her, because she played sports with other pupils who supported the Mojahedin."*

She had reason to be anxious, because a short while afterwards, in the "common" unit, I saw what they had done to her little daughter.

A little later, I don't know why, they changed our cell. We were separated. I saw a former friend, Kobra Alizadeh, from whom I had had no news for a long time. Her feet were shredded with a hole several centimetres deep. She was sitting at the end of the cell, very weak and voiceless. When she saw me, her eyes shone. Seeing her in that state, I was shocked and I needed a moment to pull myself together.

Mother Massoumeh

Massoumeh Ilekhani, a mother about thirty-six years old, was one of our cellmates. We called these women "mother" because of the respect we felt for them, and in order to make the torturers respect them.

Mother Massoumeh was quite a slender woman with a fragile little face. Calm and sedate, she seemed to us to have great endurance and patience. At first sight, her respectful behaviour attracted attention, then her hair captivated everyone's eyes. Two long plaits went down almost to her knees. I had never before seen anything like it. One of the favourite pastimes of the girls in the cell was to do her hair and plait it. It made her laugh and she let us do whatever we wanted with her hair. She was always good-tempered. We adored her.

Mother Massoumeh had been imprisoned in the Shah's time, after the birth of her son, for her sympathy with the Mojahedin. And now after the birth of her second child, eleven years later, she found herself in Khomeini's prisons. *"What a strange fate!"* she said. *"Both my children are having to grow up without their mother. Isn't it strange that I was arrested just after their birth? I'm ashamed because it's their grandmother who's having to take all the responsibility for my children."*

One day when she was praying, I noticed that she wasn't wearing socks. When she prostrated herself, I saw that she had had an operation on her feet. I was intrigued and looked at them more closely. Her toenails were either missing or deformed. When she finished praying, I gently stroked the soles of her feet. She gave a little, brief cry, quickly tucking her feet underneath her. It was obviously very painful.

"What happened to your feet?" I asked her in astonishment.

"Sh! It's nothing."

But I insisted and she confessed to me:

"It dates from the Shah's time."

She said no more and put her socks back on. Her toenails had been torn out during her torture, but she had never spoken of it. And in spite of her pain, she had hidden it from us.

She had many qualities that were characteristic of the Mojahedin. She taught us a great deal and we respected her profoundly. I owe it to her, among other things, that I learned about Khomeini's regime and know that I must never trust it.

One day, a group of mullahs, whom I did not know, started to make a tour of the cells. When they entered ours, we didn't say a word to them. *"We came to see if you had any problems because we would like to solve them,"* they told us. Mother Massoumeh forbade us to say anything to them at all. *"We have nothing to say to our enemy,"* she answered them coldly. So they left with their tails between their legs.

We later understood how right she was. It was in fact a scenario which they had perfected in order to identify the girls who complained, and eliminate them. It was a way of evaluating the prisoners, learn the weaknesses and strengths of each one and thus discover their politics.

Mother Massoumeh will always be in my eyes the symbol of those prodigious, anonymous people crushed in a massacre, whose true importance no one understood, and whose story no one knew. Massoumeh loved to speak of the heroism of the Mojahedin in the Shah's prisons and felt she was very small compared to them. She explained to us the value of what they had done.

But I am certain that in Khomeini's time there were thousands like them, and Massoumeh Ilekhani was one of them. I don't know if, after the fall of that regime, we shall find the names of all those heroes.

An adolescent full of dreams

In the cell, there was also a girl of sixteen, a brunette. She was small and slender. She was called Zahra. She too had been arrested in a street raid. As she had a few romance novels on her, the pasdaran had picked her up.

She was sentimental and travelled in her dreams. She took no interest in politics or in the world around her. She came from a poor family and hoped to marry so as to escape her poverty. But her arrest had overturned her life and all her plans.

Zahra was epileptic. The first time I saw her have a fit, I thought she was dead. First she had seizure with convulsions, then all her body contracted violently, which prevented her from breathing and, one or two minutes later, her lips and face were cyanosed. Then, horrified, I knocked on the cell door shouting: *"Come here! Someone's dying!"* The doctor came and gave her an injection. The fit stopped and her colour came back before she fell asleep.

Every time they took Zahra to be interrogated, she came back with her feet swollen and bloody. Sometimes the cable blows started a fit and she was at death's door. It was only then that they stopped.

They had absolutely no evidence against her, but they didn't set her free and this extra injustice weighed on us. I understood later that this pressure on the non-political people was deliberate. They wanted to abuse them: from spying on the other prisoners to sexual abuse …

One day, I heard two guards talking in the interrogation room. *"I asked for the girl's hand, but they refused, because I'm a pasdar"* said one. *"Bring her here and do what you like with her! After that, they'll have to give her to you!"* answered the other.

It often happened that Zahra lost patience. Then she got up, drummed on the cell door, shouted, cursed and asked why she wasn't set free. We tried to calm her because we knew she would be tortured again and she might not recover. And, systematically, the torturers took her away and sent her back to us half in a coma, her feet swollen like sausages.

In our cell, there was another girl called Nouri (Light). She came from the North and supported the Mojahedin. They came to take her every day to interrogations where she had to watch the horrible tortures practised in the basement of the prison's unit 209.

Once, they took her away and tortured her for hours, then left her there so that she could hear the shrieking of the others and see them undergoing torture. When she came back, she wasn't the same person. *"Torturers like those have never existed in the entire history. They took me to the basement. It was dark and the walls were covered with white tiles, like in slaughterhouses. Those tiles were covered in blood. I asked myself how so much blood could have been projected onto the walls, and from what body it could have come. And then I looked all round me and I saw young men hung up by their hands tied behind their backs or by their feet. Some were moaning, with their faces bloodied. Others weren't moving any longer and weren't making any noise. I really think they were dead.*

"One of them, who was hung up by his hands tied behind his back, had his face covered with blood. He opened his eyes for a few seconds and caught a glimpse of me. I thought he was looking for someone. He called out to me with a great deal of difficulty and murmured: 'Little sister! I'm very ill! I'm going to die! Tell them I didn't speak.' I didn't know what to do, my heart was going to burst. I put myself under his legs and said to him: 'Lean on my shoulders to relieve the pressure on your arms. Please lean on me!' But he wasn't willing and the only thing he managed to whisper to me was: 'I didn't speak.' I supported him with my back, but he no longer reacted."

Every day they took Zahra for a few hours into that world of horror.

In memory of the brave souls who burnt like a butterfly around a candle to expose the injustice and the atrocities of the mullahs' regime ruling Iran, I dedicate this book to people with beautiful souls and awakened conscience who do not want to see the memories of the self sacrificing butterflies forgotten.

Zobeideh and her Hezbollah family

There was another rather strange girl in the cell. It was easy to distinguish her from the others. She seemed somewhat perturbed. At first, I didn't succeed in finding out who she was. When I had settled in and made the acquaintance of my other cellmates, I found out that she was called Zobeideh and that she came from a village in the North of the country. All her family were with the Hezbollah or the pasdaran. Where she lived, her father was the head of a *committee* and whipped people. Her presence astonished me. At first I thought she was a mole, that she was there to spy on us. So I tried to find out a bit more about her. She told me that when she was at school, she befriended the boys and had sexual relations with men. When I asked her how she had been able to do that when her father whipped men and women just because they went for a walk together while unmarried, she simply answered that she made a temporary marriage! In other words, it was prostitution "legalised" by the mullahs, while normal people were being whipped for much less. Her father, her brothers and her brothers-in-law were enforcing that rule, but it was she who was its victim.

"So how do you come to be here?" I asked her. From what she told me, I understood that in that small town, this practice had raised questions about her family, who claimed to be very religious. To stop her doing any more such "silly" things, she had been sent to Tehran to stay with her sister and brother-in-law who were both with pasdaran. It was her brother-in-law who had had her locked up in Evin to frighten her. Zobeideh said that her brother-in-law worked in that prison.

Sometimes they took Zobeideh away. When she came back she said she had been interrogated. *"They are looking for one of my friends. They would like to find his family through me. But I feel sorry for him and I haven't given his address."* She was lying, she had given his name and address, but it was clear that they hadn't found him.

One day she came back particularly frightened and shocked from the interrogation. Zobeideh might have come from a family of pasdaran and "religious" people, she might have grown up in their hating environment and be used to their actions, but she was completely devastated when she saw what they did to girls, and she spoke of it to us.

That day, she had come back in a state of shock. I remember asking her why she was so upset. *"I saw my brother-in-law, it was him. I recognised his voice first of all; when I turned round, I saw that he had covered his face. He had tied a woman to the bed of torture and he was whipping her with a cable. So to check if it was really him, I looked to see if he was one-handed. Yes it was him all right. He had tied the cable round his wrist and he was hitting that woman with unbelievable force. How hard he was hitting! It was horrible. So he's a torturer too! That was what his "work" at Evin was!"*

She cried as she repeated: *"So he's a torturer too! I can't believe it!"* I asked her for her brother-in-law's name. She told me he was called Elias Baradaran, and that previously he was a student.

Zobeideh knew nothing of Khomeini's art of transforming students into torturers and human beings into monsters. A few days later, they took her away. I think she was set free because she wasn't a prisoner. It was just a family affair.

Executions at any time

In unit 209, every day about 6:00 p.m., at dinner time, we heard an enormous and deafening noise, like a lorry shedding a heavy load of metal. However much we thought about it, we couldn't understand where that noise came from, especially at sunset. We thought it must have been a building site and this idea persisted for a time.

One evening, a girl said as she came back from interrogation: *"They took away a group for execution."* That evening we heard a bigger than usual load of metal being shed. And suddenly we all cried out: *"Executions! It's the sound of executions by firing squads!"* It was the discharge of tens of firearms being fired at once on our friends.

Silence fell, heavy with pain. We were sitting in a circle with a dubious liquid supposed to be soup. We murmured the song *The Land of Martyrs*[5]:

"O Iran
"Land of martyrs
"Land of the eternal lions
"I waited a long time
"To be a Mojahed
"I sacrificed my life
"At dawn
"For the people of Iran"

We had read in novels that prisoners were executed on the scaffold at daybreak, but as Khomeini's regime executed at any time of day – it had no sort of importance for them – and we were ignorant of this, we therefore waited in anguish for dawn, in all innocence.

---

5. An old song of the People's Mojahedin dating from the time of the Shah's prisons, very popular in Iran.

Nobody was eating, we were all silent, our heads down. I saw Zahra's spoon move trembling towards her plate, great tears falling into her soup. Like an automaton, she carried her spoon to her mouth and cried with all her being.

When we had finished singing, we collected ourselves. I asked one of the girls to give me a leg up to climb up to the window at the top of the wall. Perhaps I might be able to hear or see something. But there was a wall opposite us and I couldn't see anything. We only heard the fatal shots. That day, we counted up to 120 coups de grâce... A hundred and twenty people slaughtered!

It had become a daily task: the firing, the singing of *The Land of Martyrs* and then climbing up to the window to try to count the fatal shots. The evening when they executed mother Kabiri (a famous political prisoner of the Shah's time, Mojahedin candidate to the Tehran legislative, who counts as one of the heroes of the Resistance in Khomeini's prisons), we counted over 220 fatal blows.

It is impossible for me to describe in what a state we found ourselves when we counted them, one after the other, knowing that every gunshot signified the death of a sister, the death of Touba, of Fahimeh, of Nahid and all those whom I so loved. When the number reached 50, 60, 80, 100 victims and we didn't know when it would stop, we had our hearts in our mouths. The sound of every bullet vibrated in the depths of our being and we felt as if our skulls would burst. And when silence came at last, we knew that the Beast was still hungry and that it was groaning. And tomorrow, whose turn will it be? How many others will be executed? I have read many books about the concentration camps: more often than not the executioners killed their victims in gas chambers, where they sent them on the pretext of making them take a shower.

At Evin and in Khomeini's other prisons, they shredded human beings first, then they kept them for days, weeks, months, even years in the claws of death. They murdered prisoners' dearest relatives under their eyes and, in the end, they killed the prisoners. It's not without reason that Ashraf Rajavi[6] had said before her death: *"The world never learned what the Iranian people lived through."*

During that period, I communicated in various ways with Tahmineh and I knew that she was well. She was in a cell in the corridor beside ours. At the times when I thought there was nobody there, I called her with a brief whistle and she answered in the same way. I had also heard her once or twice when she was arguing with some pasdaran. She was still just as persevering, courageous and full of life. Once she started imitating the sound of a frog, which made us laugh a lot. I knew it was her because that was one of the funny things she did when we were students. But there, this provoked the anger of the pasdaran. They entered the cell, yelling, and covered us with insults.

The mere fact of having irritated them delighted us. At every chance, one of us tried to do it to them. The guards kept watch to find out who it was, and if they caught the one responsible, they tortured her. But in spite of everything, the girls didn't give up, because in the end, it was a form of resistance to spread joy in that hellish place of death. That was why we went on doing it. I was simply glad to know that Tahmineh was alive.

---

6. First wife of Massoud Rajavi, she was struck down in Tehran on 8 February 1982 when her home was attacked by the pasdaran.

The little Indian girl

Kobra Alizadeh was one of the girls in my cell. She was a former classmate of mine. She was quiet, very hard working, and everyone adored her.

When she was a student, she had long shining hair. She dressed it in two plaits. Her cheekbones were high and her skin matt. We had nicknamed her "the Indian girl". In the dormitory of nursing school, we sometimes amused ourselves by tying a band around her head and dancing around her in the Indian manner.

Now the little Indian was in front of me, in the cell, with her feet in tatters; but the spark she always had, that spark of love still shone in her eyes.

Kobra had also been arrested in the street. At the time of her arrest, she had managed to swallow the documents she had on her and the pasdaran hadn't been able to seize them. That's why they felt a savage hatred for her. They had immediately started torturing her and torn her feet to shreds, which prevented her from walking for a long time.

When I saw her, she was a little better and could walk with the help of other people, putting her weight partially on the sides of her feet. They were infected and we had no means of taking care of her. The state of her feet undoubtedly made a skin graft necessary. *"They won't operate on me,"* she declared. *"My torturer said that I was condemned to death because I come from the North."*

The pasdaran felt a strange hatred towards the Northern people. *"The Northern people,"* they declared, *"are all counter-revolutionaries because in the North there are more supporters of the Mojahedin than anywhere else."* Kobra said that as soon as she had arrived in the torture chamber, the torturer had announced: *"I am going to start by giving you a hundred blows because you're from the North,"* and he had whipped her without stopping. Then, he had let out in a whisper: *"Now I'm going to hit you on your own account."*

"And then I spat in his face," said Kobra with great determination.

Only the person who has spent a few hours in the regime's torture chambers , even if he or she has only had five or six lashes, can understand what it means to spit in the face of the torturer, especially after a hundred lashes.

They took Kobra away again several time and whipped her on the wounds in her feet.

"I was able to see Tahmineh and I just had time to tell her I was with you," she confided to me one day when she was coming back from being tortured.

"Do you think you could see her again?"

"Perhaps."

Then I wrote a letter to Tahmineh on a little piece of paper and asked Kobra to give it to her with her own hand if she passed her again.

I must make it clear that in Khomeini's prisons there is no possibility of being able to write, still less when under torture. During an interrogation, I had stolen a fountain-pen nib and a few sheets of paper that I hid under the upper ledge of the window of our cell. We used them on occasions of that sort.

I thought it would be better for me if I also had a letter on me in case I met Tahmineh. In this correspondence, I told her about my situation and the arrests and gave her news and information. I had rolled up the paper in my pocket and I waited for a chance. Then an opportunity arose.

Zahra often had fits under the shower. One day when she was there with Zobeideh, we suddenly heard violent blows on the door. A pasdar shouted: *"Hengameh must come quickly!"* I put on all that I owned because that kind of summons was often one with no return. *"Follow me quickly!"* ordered the pasdar when I came out. We passed through a passage at the back, and he opened the door of a cell with no ceiling. In fact it was the unit's exercise yard.

I saw Zobeideh sitting by the head of Zahra who was stretched on the ground, cyanosed.

"She's dying. There's no doctor, so I called you," she whispered to me as soon as she saw me.

"What should I do?" asked the guard.

"Bring a syringe and an injection of valium!" I answered.

And he went off to look for them. In the yard, the first thing I noticed was the linen drying on a line, and above all Tahmineh's tunic with its brown and cream checks.

"Hold her head like that," I called out to Zobeideh.

I got up and slid the message I had in my pocket into the pocket in Tahmineh's tunic. I thanked the Lord a thousand times for having given me that chance. After the injection, Zahra's condition improved and her colour came back. When the guard saw that, he said: *"We've someone else who isn't well. You might examine her, because we don't know when the doctor will come."* He led me into another cell where there was a pregnant woman. She had been tortured and was in a bad state. I asked the guard to fetch some sugared water, and until he came back I spoke to the patient. When she trusted me, she told me that they had shown her a heap of flesh deformed by torture and told her it was her husband. She was still in shock.

"She's pregnant and seriously ill," I told the guard who had come back. *"Bring her some jam, some milk or that sort of thing."*

The strangest thing was that he went to fetch them. It must be said that that guard was an exception: he was cognizant of sins and faults in his religious beliefs.

The girls knew the times when he was on duty and were able to get quite a few things through him. For example, we had some milk, sugar and other goods for the wounded. But it didn't last long, he was transferred.

To return to Kobra's story, she left our unit a little later. In fact, she was taken away to be executed, but we didn't know it. We only found out when we transferred to the common unit.

The little Indian girl, with her lovely smile, went back to God. She was executed in the most complete silence and injustice, without her family knowing where she was or what had happened to her. She was murdered but she disappointed her executioners who wanted to see her break faith. I learned afterwards that her young brother was executed a little later, in the North.

A couple of heroes

One day when we were sitting in the cell, they opened the door and pushed in a woman wearing a hospital smock. She had a little towel on her head instead of a headscarf. She was pale and seemed exhausted. We stood up immediately to take her arm and help her to sit down. Once she had sat down, the towel was pushed aside to show a pretty young face. She had shining brown eyes and a long forehead. Her mouth was terribly bruised or, more precisely, burst, which made her incapable of speech. She tried to greet us and thank us with a slight smile and glowing eyes. We quickly put warm clothes on her and prepared some sugared water, because in the state her mouth was in, she could eat nothing; in any event, we had nothing else.

We let her rest for a little, then we told her that we were being accused of being supporters of the People's Mojahedin. It was the practice in prison to give our political position without any specific details, because the regime had put moles among us. They spied on us and made reports to the torturers. We were therefore careful and avoided giving too many details. In spite of everything, while taking all possible precautions, we gave our interlocutresses all the necessary information and they didn't ask too many questions either, because they knew the value of any detail given under torture.

The new arrival was called Afsaneh Afzalniya, and her husband was Abbas Pishdadiyan. From what I remember, she was a student of social sciences and they had a six-month old daughter, Fatemeh. The pasdaran had recognised them in Mossadegh Street. As they had resisted arrest, they had been severely wounded. They had been transported first of all to the hospital to be treated. At the end of three days, the pasdaran had taken them to Evin prison to interrogate them by torture.

As she could eat nothing, Afsaneh was very weak. Our appeals to obtain some milk or food that she could swallow had been in vain. We gave her sugared water or the small amount of sauce they served us. But even those liquids burned her because of the wounds on her lips and in her mouth. She swallowed only very little with a thousand and one difficulties. In spite of that, her torturers didn't let go of her and went on torturing her.

"They ask me for an address in Tajrish (a quarter in north Tehran) *that I don't know. That's why they're torturing me."*

She told us that, in the hope that one day the news would reach the Resistance, the People's Mojahedin, so that they would know that she had kept the secret of the house in Tajrish, and so that they could evacuate it if necessary. We pretended not to understand, which was the rule in prison.

One day, coming back from her interrogation, she was very sad but at the same time seemed determined. Her eyes were full of tears.

"They are wild beasts. They took me to see my husband. He was unrecognisable. He was bathed in his own blood. I don't know what they did to him to make him bleed like that. His hands, his fingers, his toes, his head, his face, his mouth, everything was in tatters and covered in blood. The torturer dragged me up to him shouting: 'That's your husband! If you want him to live, speak! Give the Tajrish address!'

Her husband had given nothing away, not one detail. Suddenly, he opened his eyes a little and in the middle of all that blood, by his looking, gave Afsaneh the signal to understand that he was strong and the regime knew nothing.

"I have no address to give you," she had the force to murmur. *"Dirty hypocrite!"*

The insult fell together with a blow of unusual violence, then she came back to the cell.

Another time, coming back from her interrogation, Afsaneh went to sit down, her head against the wall, then she described the pain devouring her body. They had put her six-month old daughter, Fatemeh, in the corridor opposite. For six days she had eaten nothing and been deprived of her mother. She no longer had enough strength even to cry. From time to time Fatemeh let a feeble moan escape her.

"*They've put her there on purpose to make me crack, to force me to sell my people because of my maternal feelings, but I won't do it, not even at the price of my child's life, I won't be a traitor.*"

And great tears rolled down her cheeks without stopping.

They executed Afsaneh twenty days after her arrest. She hadn't given away a single detail. Later, a girl who knew her told me: "*Afsaneh wrung her enemies' necks. She frustrated them terribly. They never knew that she had a very responsible post in the Mojahedin, otherwise they wouldn't have executed her so quickly.*"

During this short period, Afsaneh had taught us a great deal, especially about traitors and spies. The regime used them to weaken the prisoners and break their resistance. The tactics had been proved a failure with the Mojahedin and had produced the opposite effect.

The regime didn't spare its efforts. Thus it transmitted the interview with a traitor through loudspeakers. Afsaneh then turned to us and called out: "*Watch out, girls, the traitor's worse than the enemy. The aim of a traitor is to break your spirit; don't believe him.*"

Given her condition, speaking was a true ordeal for Afsaneh. But with a choice between her own interest and the resistance, she chose the resistance. It was only when she was certain that we had truly understood and that we would make no mistake that she calmed down.

They drew Afsaneh from the cell a few days before finishing her off. We don't know where they took her or what they did to her. It was later on when I found out about her execution.

It was also some time since I had had any news of Tahmineh. Since I had heard her confronting the pasdaran, she had no longer answered to the usual whistle.

They had taken me to be interrogated. I didn't know that in fact it was the last series. They had blindfolded me with my own headscarf. Discreetly, I had taken advantage of a moment's inattention to adjust it so that I could see and I distinguished my two torturers.

They asked me the same questions and I gave the same answers. I saw their gestures from under my blindfold, but they didn't know that.

"Tahmineh has told everything! She said you were in contact with X and Y."

"It's a lie, you've made it all up! If you're telling the truth, then go and find Tahmineh!"

I knew they were talking rubbish, but I wanted to make them to let me meet Tahmineh.

"She has been transferred elsewhere," said one of them after exchanging a few words with the other torturer. *"Would you recognise her writing?"*

"Yes!"

They brought the record of her evidence. It was certainly her writing. It was the false information of which she had told me, unknown first names without surnames, with a ridiculous and confused sketch. All that proved to me that they knew nothing or that they were bluffing.

"It's a lie," I exclaimed, throwing myself about, *"I don't know those people, you must bring Tahmineh!"*

"Shut up! Stop it! We'll bring Tahmineh to you and then we'll deal with you."

They were lying and, a little later, I was transferred to the common unit 246.

Part Three

The first year in prison

The transfer

In general, we were judged in unit 209, and then we were transferred elsewhere. But this didn't happen in my case. I was transferred in December or January to unit 246, the lower floor, room 4. It had been three months in all that I had been in unit 209, but I hadn't had any visits. Yet my family knew where I was, thanks to those who had been freed.

To reach unit 246 it was necessary at first to cross a space at the top of the steps where the pasdaran women of the unit were lodged. Then after going down about twenty steps, you reached the warders' lodge. Following the left-hand wall, you came to the door which led to the unit's corridor. It had metal bars and, except at the time for exercise, it was always bolted.

The corridor was L-shaped. In one wing were rooms 1, 2, 3 and 4 and the shower. After turning left, there were two lavatories, then rooms 5 and 6. In each one, two windows opened onto the exercise area. The upper floor of the unit had the same shape. They had crammed in an average of 60 to 100 people in each room. The first two were smaller than the others. In fact there were five times as many of us as there was room for. The first thing that caught the eye was the excessive overcrowding of the prison.

There was always a long queue in front of the lavatories because, out of the two rows of WCs consisting of eight lavatories, only two worked. Which amounted to two WCs for 500 people.

On my arrival in the unit, everyone greeted me. I had to step over the people sitting in the corridor to reach room number 4. I went in and put down the few things I owned in a corner. Then I went out again. In fact, I wanted to know whether I knew anyone. I saw Afkham in the queue for the lavatories. We behaved as if we didn't know each other. I had known her at the association and we had seen each other at the hospital. She came to our home as well when we had get-togethers.

After a few minutes she came to see me. We had a chat. She told me she hadn't been betrayed and they knew nothing about her. She was pregnant when they arrested her and, under the torture known as "football" where the victim was used as a kicking ball, she had miscarried. She told me the rules of the unit and put me on my guard against the spies and suspect girls.

Tahmineh's execution

In the corridor, a young, small girl came up to me.

"They were calling you Hengameh. Are you a nurse?"
"Yes!"
"Are you Tahmineh's friend?" she joyfully asked.
"Yes! Have you some news?" I asked, full of hope.
The axe fell: *"She's been executed."*

I had the impression that I was being sucked into a void. I could no longer feel my legs, I couldn't control my knees. I felt them fold, and sat down, leaning against the wall. I don't know how long I remained knocked flat. My brain no longer functioned.

"*I thought you knew,*" she said miserably.

"*No! It's nothing,*" I said at last when I was able to control myself. "*Tell me what happened. How do you know my name?*"

"*My name is Mahshid; I was in the same cell as Tahmineh. One day she picked up the linen she had left to dry. Once she was dressed, she pulled a rolled-up piece of paper from her pocket. And then when she'd read it, she shook her head, laughing, and cried out: 'Hengameh!' It was you who had sent her the letter. She tore it into little bits and threw it into the lavatory to make it disappear. And then she said to me: 'It's Hengameh, my friend. She was worried about me. She's sent me a letter.*"

She told me that Tahmineh was very happy and full of life.

"*Once, she started imitating a frog sound to amuse a poor woman who had been arrested by mistake, so that she shouldn't worry about her situation. They beat her until the morning and kept her in the cold. When she came back, she was all pale and trembling. Her torturer was harrassing her, I don't know what he wanted, he wouldn't let go of her.*

"*One day he came into the cell with a paper in his hand. 'Either you consent to the interview, or you take this paper and make your will.' With a smile on her lips and without taking her eyes off the torturer, Tahmineh stood up and without a word tore the paper out of his hands. Then she came back and sat down. The torturer was very annoyed, gave her a kick and cursed her before he left, slamming the door.*

"Tahmineh wrote her will with the same smile and saluted us, one after the other. An hour afterwards, they came to fetch her to be executed."

Not having had any news for a month, and even though I had guessed she had been executed, I couldn't believe it. Perhaps I wanted to console myself. I couldn't believe that all that joy of living, that love and that intelligence no longer existed. In our profession, we do everything to keep an incurable invalid alive for a few more minutes. And there, all those people, the best people, in good health, young and full of life, were disappearing, killed or torn to pieces because of the mediaeval, selfish and autocratic convictions of a bloodthirsty old man, Khomeini. Why? It was a question that remained unanswered.

Little Fati

One or two days after my arrival in the common unit, a girl who was overflowed with energy came to see me.

"You've come from 209?"

"Yes!"

"Have you any news of my mother? Her name is Tal'at."

"Fatemeh! You're Fatemeh?!" I said, suddenly remembering mother Tal'at's anxiety for her daughter.

"You were with my mummy? You saw her?" she cried out, flinging her arms round my neck. She couldn't keep still, she was exploding with joy.

"Your mummy was set free. She was anxious about you, I'm sure she's looking for you," I told her.

She replied: "They arrested me a day after my mother and brought me here. My torturer's terrible to me. He never stops repeating that he's going to kill me."

"Not at all! He's just trying to frighten you," I said.

She was really too young to be executed just because she'd played sport or for any other asinine reason.

I had made friends with Fatemeh. I felt that she wanted to compensate for her mother's absence. She talked to me, joked, shared her worries, asked my advice, slept by my side, took my hand and held it until she fell asleep. In short, she didn't let me go. I loved her too. I understood her needs and tried to help her. Every time she went to be interrogated, she told me that her torturer was threatening her.

In spite of everything, she went on doing silly things in the unit, childish things, and that's why the girls called her "Fati the mouse", because she was little and quick-moving like a mouse, and also because her family name lent itself to that: Mousha'i – *Moush* in Persian means mouse.

When they came to execute her

One day, before noon, the loudspeaker called out the names of Zahra Hessami, Fatemeh Mousha'i and another girl. Hearing those names, especially that of Fatemeh, I collapsed; it was as if I had been tetanised, or electrocuted. I didn't want to believe it. I looked at the others to see whether I had heard properly. But I had!

A heavy silence fell in the unit. Everyone knew that they had been summoned for execution. Zahra rose, smiling, and greeted the girls who were weeping in silence.

Zahra was a student at the university of industrial sciences. She was a well-conducted, calm girl who always laughed at my jokes. She encouraged me to avoid sinking into silence and to do everything to improve the atmosphere. She incited us to work together, to do sports and singing.

I could no longer move. She came up and shook me.

"You haven't the right to cry," she said, wiping away my tears. *"Remember, you must always laugh, not let silence overcome the others, don't forget! The enemy mustn't see our sadness."*

And she left.

But Fati!... I saw her run into the room with her shoes in her hand, having difficulty in keeping her veil on her head. She threw her arms around my neck, hugging me in her little arms, full of joy.

"We're going to Ghezel Hessar prison. We're being transferred. If only you could come too."

"Yes, you're being transferred to Ghezel Hessar," I tried to say with a smile.

She ran out towards the stairs. I didn't have the courage to follow her, to look at her. All of a sudden I heard moaning and weeping from girls who were saying her name. Behind the door, I leaned against the door and then I let myself slide towards the ground. I no longer held back the sobs that choked me. I never understood her bloodthirsty executioner who had vented his animal hatred on that little girl.

As she was running towards the stairs, she was touched by doubt because of the silence and the sadness of the girls. Before she came to the staircase door, she turned round, looked more attentively at the girls and suddenly she understood.

"NO!" Her cry rang out. *"No, I don't want to die! I don't want to die!"* And she fainted. She was far too young to be ready to die. She hadn't yet smelt the scent of life.

Khomeini's brutal animals took her away, unconscious, dragging her on the ground. They left behind them
the stifled cries of the girls: *"Fati! Fati! No! No!"*

Through my sobs I cried out in the depths of my being: *"But why? Monsters! Even in your barbarous law, what
had that little girl done to be executed? You bloodthirsty animals!"*

My little Fati was still thirsty for her mother's love and
tenderness. My God, but why? Why?

Thoughts in prison

In prison, your moments are like none of those in ordinary
life. They seem to touch another dimension of being, of
existence, of life, of injustice, of honour, of love, of hatred,
of everything in short. You cannot find those thoughts in
any books, or in any film, or even in all your life. It is only
in prison that you can grasp their meaning.

These painful thoughts in prison come when you can't
and won't accept that little Fati was executed. When you
call her, and hear no answer. The sound of her laughter
rings in your ears, the image of her innocent look appears
to you like a living reality, but when you hold out your
hand to her, she disappears. When you want to dispel her
fear of solitude and separation from her mother, you want
to stroke her lovely plaits and wipe away her tears, she isn't
there any more. When sleeping, you feel her little arm in
yours, you really feel it. Between dream and reality, for a
moment or several moments, you think that the sight of
them taking Fati away to be executed was just a nightmare,
and that she's still there, just beside you. You want to make
sure of it, you stretch out your hand to touch her and feel

the warmth of her body, and all of a sudden the bitter reality strikes you. No! The truth is that Fati is gone. The truth is that Fati was executed. My tiny little girl, in what tomb do you rest? Whose hand did you take? Are you no longer afraid?

When we were joking, we looked at Zahra to rejoice in her smile; suddenly we pull ourselves back because she's no longer there. In her place there is another Zahra. She may leave too, tomorrow, or sooner than tomorrow. When we walk in the yard measuring two metres by three, in the sunless cold, we look in front of us, behind us, she is everywhere. During our walks, we used to walk together. We don't manage to feel that she's absent, although reality tells us the opposite. It's as if she were walking beside you, as if she were repeating these words with you.

These are prison thoughts that you can only understand in prison.

There was a great crowd in the unit and we had to sleep by turns. That was the problem at night. People squashed up like sardines beside each other and we still lacked sufficient space. One group waited, standing or sitting. When the others woke up, they laid down. We reserved a few extra centimetres for the mothers and the wounded in the corner of the room. But it didn't make much difference.

There was no peace to be found there. In addition to the interrogations and physical tortures for each prisoner, there was a psychological torture common to all the prisoners. At 4 in the morning, brutally, the unit's loudspeakers howled religious chants in the insufferable voice of Ahangaran, one of the regime's singers, at full volume. It made everyone jump, the children started to cry, our hearts beat too fast for at least a few minutes, then, blocking up our ears and covering our heads, we tried to go back to sleep. That miserable noise went on without stopping until the evening.

In the morning, for breakfast, they brought a pot of tea with bromide - which acts as a tranquiliser - and the girl on duty in each unit went to fetch the tea with some pans.

The food

Given that the interrogation period was over for most of the girls, we might have expected an improvement in the conditions of our detention. Far from it.

For example, as to food, we were really under pressure. We were always hungry and were given just enough not to die, but we were never able to eat our fill. For breakfast, there was a piece of bread the size of a hand, ten grammes of cheese, and a glass of tepid, insipid tea. Well, even out of that little bit, they managed to leave something out. One day it was the cheese, another, the bread, on yet another, it was the sugar. In short, they didn't let us eat even that little ration in peace.

For lunch and dinner, things weren't better. Sticky rice or a little thin soup with nothing in it, or a purée of beans and chick peas. And so little even of that! As to the cutlery and the plates, there weren't any, just a few trays on which they served the meals. Each tray was for a certain number of people. For example, when someone new arrived in the unit, the person in charge of the room assigned her to a group. The grouping of the prisoners depended on the meal trays. We had to eat with our hands or to use a common spoon; we had got used to it.

One day, we were served a dish that was supposed to be rice with chicken. In fact, there was only chicken skin, and that was spoiled. Perhaps that was deliberate. Within five hours, 500 people had food poisoning. With the diarrhoea and vomiting fits, the situation was catastrophic, because there were only two WCs and the girls were writhing with pain as they queued. Some of them, however, who were very ill indeed, couldn't wait. Those who were less ill had to make way for them. Some of them were on the verge of death.

At first, the torturers didn't take the situation seriously, but when they saw that it was affecting everyone and spreading to other units, after several hours, they finally took action. But they couldn't put everyone in hospital, as all the units were affected. Apart from a few who were very ill, we all stayed in the units. They distributed some yoghurt and a few medicaments. The girls who were between life and death were sent to the infirmary. There were some deaths, but we never knew how many, nor who they were.

The food situation for the children, and especially the babies, was really catastrophic. We had no baby food, and they didn't give us any powdered milk either. They said: *"It's better for the children of the Mojahedin to die."* The poor mothers strained their ingenuity to devise products based on sugared water and crumbs of dry bread. Ahmad-Reza, a little boy aged one, contracted tuberculosis and they were forced to give him to his grandmother.

Children's situation was a perpetual problem because the jailors didn't give them back to their families. Since the parents had been arrested in the street, the regime didn't want the families to learn about it. I understood the reason later on: they could then get rid of people without being held accountable. If they had let parents or near relatives know from the beginning about the arrests, they wouldn't have been able to eliminate their victims so easily. That's what happened to many people who disappeared and whose traces were never found.

Hygiene

In January or February 1982, they cut off the weekly two hours of hot water, claiming that the water-heater was broken. All our protests were in vain. We were deprived of hot water for two months and the water in Evin prison, high in the mountains, was so icy that washing one plate was enough to turn your fingers blue. So as to showering ...

Because of this, the unit swarmed with lice and we were forced to use DDT. We powdered our heads and clothes with it. The children, the babies and the old people were in a disastrous state, their bodies eaten up. We protested several times with no result, the pasdaran women laughed at us saying *"Go on, resist!"* We then agreed that those who had visitors would tell their families. So all the girls spoke of it on the same visit day, because if the news was related to the families on various days, the regime would have discovered the plan and would have forbidden visits.

We told our families that our shower had been cut off and that the units were being invaded by lice. Our relations therefore protested with spirit and all, collectively, complained wherever they could. When the torturers saw that the affair was going to spread outside the prisons, they were forced to open the hot-water tap again. But this victory was dearly bought. We knew very well that we should have to pay for it with tortures and above all with the execution of those whom the regime had called the "brains" of this protest.

By this kind of action, the regime wanted to intensify the pressure and wear the prisoners out. It took pleasure in giving the captives trouble.

Everything was a good excuse for suppression: forbidding visits, not distributing meals, not giving any medicaments or milk to the babies, confiscating the Qu'rans and other religious books and even the government newspapers. They even went as far as stopping us from talking, with the excuse that we were getting organised. There was a whole heap of other actions like that.

The old prisoners

Among the prisoners were a few old and ill people who couldn't look after themselves. They had been arrested on the pretext that they were rich or had Zoroastrian beliefs[1], and this constituted an additional stress for the prisoners. These elderly and sick individuals were in addition to the Mojahedin mothers arrested either for their activities or those of their children.

One of those women was called Mrs. Kotobi. She was accused of being rich. Later on, we learned that the regime wanted to get hold of her houses without her heirs having any say in it. That was why the pasdaran had thrown her into prison in spite of her state of health. She absolutely couldn't look after herself. Caring for her in that overcrowded and unhygienic unit was a real problem. We had no hot water, or only had some for two hours a week. In

---

1. Religion of the Persians before Islam.

fact, after the first quarter of an hour, the water became almost tepid. That's why we put the children and the old people first, and the others afterwards: ten minutes for thirty people.

In these conditions, taking care of an old lady was really frustrating. If we didn't care for her, she smelt. Where could we put her in a place where people lived squashed like sardines? The poor thing complained and cried continually. She begged God incessantly: *"Lord, come to my help!"*

One day, she was at death's door. She fell into a coma, with irregular breathing. Mother Tavanaïn-Fard stretched her out in the position of prayer and began to intone the Qur'an. We called the pasdaran women urgently. As they didn't react, we shouted curses at them to make them take that poor woman to the infirmary.

After a few days, when she was better, she was sent back to our unit. After that, she didn't want to eat. Perhaps she wanted to let herself die. Being a nurse, I often took care of her. I stayed beside her so that she shouldn't feel alone. She made me sad. After all those years of effort and suffering, when she was on the point of death, she found herself alone in the claws of those monsters, far from her family. And they didn't set her free. She could have spent her last days with her own family.

Thinking she had dropped her guard, I gave her something to drink with a spoon. She moved her lips a little and felt the water. She gently lifted her bony, icy hand, took mine, then opened her misty eyes. She looked at me and said weakly: *"Bless you! Pray for me to die soon!"* And I prayed God to save her. Mrs. Kotobi remained in that state for a long time, without any change for the better. One day, at last, they came to fetch her. I don't know what happened to her.

The old Mojahedin mothers

The account of the tortures inflicted on Mojahedin mothers is a story in itself. The torturers gave proof of limitless cruelty towards them. Those mothers were a considerable weight in prison, especially when the pasdaran women allowed themselves to do certain things. The mothers often became human shields of the girls and roared like lionesses.

Mother Mohammadi was one of them. Lajevardi, the chief torturer at Evin, felt an indescribable hatred for her. It derived from the fact that mother Mohammadi's son was none other than Ibrahim Zakeri, who had a position of high responsibility among the Mojahedin. Lajevardi put no limits on the insults and injuries he inflicted on her.

As that mother knew about his past, she spoke to him very contemptuously and ridiculed him in front of the other prisoners. That's why Lajevardi avoided public confrontations with her. She used to say to him: *"So, Assadollah[2], do you remember that you used to boast that the Mojahedin knew you and that you were proud that they spoke to you? What's happening to you now? Why do you murder them like Yazid[3]? Shame on you!"*

One day when the mother was praying, a pasdar named Rahele, who was the daughter of mullah Moussavi Tabrizi, the chief torturer of Tabriz city, came to taunt us in the unit. Just to have something to say, she began to

---

2. The torturer Lajevardi's first name.

3. A historical reference to the silent partner in the assassination of Hussein, the third Shi'ite Imam and grandson of the prophet Muhammad.

criticise the way the mother prayed.

The mother, who had been watching her out of the corner of her eye from the moment she arrived in the unit, ended her prayer, then took her old shoe in her hand and rushed towards her shouting: *"You dirty whore! You think you're going to teach me Islam?!"*

The astonished pasdar panicked. She hastily opened the door of the unit and, shamefaced, fled up the stairs two at a time. The mother threw a volley of curses after her.

It was because she resisted and because she believed deeply in the values and fundamental principles of the Mojahedin that Lajevardi attacked her personally. He tortured and executed her himself. There were no bounds that Lajevardi didn't break in torturing mother Mohammadi and mother Kabiri.

I had never seen Lajevardi close up. I had seen him in photographs and I had glimpsed him from afar during speeches at Evin. One day, I no longer remember why, he came into our unit. He went from room to room threatening the prisoners. And then he stopped in front of the door of our room and, there, I was able to see him at close range. Never, no, never have I seen such a repulsive beast; not even in the cinema. He was abominably ugly. When he took off his glasses to wipe them, I observed his eyes: they were like two globes full of black blood. His expression was indescribable. However hard I try, I can't find an adequate term for it. He seemed like a contemptible snake. My mother used to say that no human being is ugly, but that God causes the depths of the soul to be reflected in the face. Lajevardi is the best possible illustration of my mother's belief.

There was nothing human in either his appearance or his face. He was a flesh and blood monster.

Compulsory Hosseinyeh[4] and Ershad[5]

In the evening, we had to go to Hosseinyeh and the whole unit was emptied. If anyone didn't go, they would knew what awaited them. This was one of the tricks invented by Lajevardi. That monster had renamed the prison, a place of torture and massacre, "the university". He wanted to pass himself off as the head of a university. Hosseinyeh had therefore become a section of that *"faculty"*! Some evenings, the pasdaran forced the prisoners to be present at parodies of Hosseinyeh.

Once, for example, they had brought a young mullah to, as they put it, *"have a free discussion, advise us and guide us on the right path"*: that of betrayal and opportunism.

The prisoners stayed there, looking at him, keeping their self-control, without saying a word. Not one question, no debate. The more that fool of a mullah tried to make someone speak, the less he managed to. Sometimes their agents asked questions, to create an atmosphere, break the resistance. But it was useless.

At first, those orators were turbaned mullahs. Then when they noticed that they achieved nothing and that the girls hated them, they brought in preachers without turbans, so as to provoke less disgust among the prisoners. Band of ignoramuses! They thought they were dealing with people like themselves and not with women who had freely chosen their path. It happened that, to break the prison-

---

4. Place of religious instruction.

5. Education.

ers' spirit, they brought in women who had repented, who were usually destined for execution, nevertheless. They underwent a pseudo-interview.

One day, too, Lajevardi tried to intervene in the Hosseinyeh. But his speech was nothing but a bunch of insults.

The whipping ration

Among us there were prisoners who were entitled to a whiping ration every day, which is to say that every evening they were taken to be interrogated and whipped until dawn. Then they were sent back to us, with their feet bloody and swollen. Then the girls took turns to massage their feet to soothe the pain and œdema. The next time, the suffering would be less atrocious and the appearance of wounds would be delayed.

The whipping ration is one of the worst tortures, because it seems endless. Every day brings its exact portion of lashes. When that is tirelessly repeated and that the lash of the whip bites on the previous day's wounds, you need the strength of a mountain to resist.

In our unit, there were two girls who had whipping rations. They were called Mina Izadi and Zahra Shab-Zendeh-Dar. I don't know why the pasdaran had decided that they must torture them every evening.

Mina was a girl of medium height with rather light brown hair and freckled all over. In spite of her daily whipping ration, she laughed all the time, joked with the girls and didn't let the night's torture affect the others.

Zahra, also a student, was very resolute. When out walking, she hopped gently to diminish the œdema on her feet. She prepared herself for the next rain of lashes and said with aplomb: *"That torturer's an imbecile, frankly, he's an idiot! He thinks that by beating us with cables, he can force us to repent, to say 'no' to the truth. So he'll never understand that it's impossible! You'd think he's condemned to live in eternal ignorance. That's why I say he's an imbecile. The regime's sure to be looking for that sort of person. I think that such idiots are rare pearls."*

The first month of Ramadan in prison, the month of fasting, arrived. We hoped that because of the sacred character of that month, our torturers would interrupt Mina's and Zahra's whipping rations. But that wasn't the case. It became clear that we didn't know them well enough and that we knew still less how religion worked for them. The religion in which Khomeini and his monsters believed never touched mercy or love. Khomeini's religion and faith exalted only hate and cruelty, which made the path to torture easy for his disciples.

That's how they came to fetch Zahra and Mina just at the moment when the fast was to be broken and they only sent them back at dawn. We waited anxiously for their return, hoping they would arrive in time for their meal, that is to say before the break of day which marks the beginning of fasting. But when they came back, their feet swollen, their eyes hollow, their lips dry and their faces pale, they no longer had the strength to eat and, as soon as they sat down, weariness overcame them.

They executed Mina in 1982 and Zahra during the massacre of political prisoners in 1988.

Nahid's mysterious dream

One day, we heard people at the entrance to the unit. We understood at once that they were bringing in a new pris-

oner. We were all curious to see her. At the entrance, two
girls helped her, supporting her because she couldn't walk
on her own. The prisoners, who were sitting or lying down
in the corridor, pushed each other aside to let her pass. She
came into our room. We made room for her in a corner
in order to spare her being in a place where people were
passing and where it was a risk of treading on her feet; they
were swollen with blood. She had haematomas up to her
thighs. A deep wound deformed the sole of one foot. Little
and thin, she had matt skin and beautiful hazel eyes. Her
face showed remarkable innocence. She thanked the girls
who came in little groups to greet her, ask after her health
and chat. She was called Nahid Izad-Khah.

Later on, when we knew one another better, she
said she was the sister of Massoud Izad-Khah, husband of
Massoumeh Azdanlou[6]. When he was arrested, Massoud
had resisted with ferocity and been cut down, but Massoumeh, who was pregnant, had been captured.

All those who had been arrested had been transferred
to unit 209 where they had been tortured. That was where
Nahid's feet had been so torn to shreds that she had to be
sent to the infirmary to have several operations. They had
grafted flesh and skin taken from her body in the place of
that which had been torn out by the lashes. Which they
didn't generally do for those condemned to death ... We
therefore hoped that they would let her live.

"The saddest moment for me," she told us, *"was when
they took me to see Massoumeh. She was alone, abandoned,
lying on the floor of her cell, her jaw broken, without any care*

---

6. Massoumeh Azdanlou was the sister of Maryam Rajavi, President-elect of the
National Council of Resistance of Iran.

or anything to eat. The smell of blood and infection stank the room out. As a gesture of cruelty, that brute of a torturer gave her a kick in the jaw. She was just able to moan. She couldn't even move."

As she shook her head, great tears accompanied every word she spoke and we wept with her. They executed Massoumeh, wounded and exhausted, and the child she was expecting.

As a result of torture, Nahid's feet had become a strange shape. After a month, the skin of her leg peeled off like a stocking from the top of the thigh. For a long time it was impossible for her to walk; she needed help to make the smallest movement.

One morning upon waking up, Nahid looked strangely joyful.

"I want to take a shower," she announced.

"But there's no hot water, the water's frozen!" we answered in amazement.

"I must go there. I must prepare to die. Last night, I dreamt that my mother was putting my hand in that of my brother Massoud and entrusting me to him. Today, I shall go to him."

The girls remained dumbstruck, not knowing what to do or say. It was only a dream after all. But Nahid took a shower, with astonishing assurance and in spite of the frozen water. Then she said her prayer and distributed everything she possessed. She put on her best clothes and waited. Suddenly, to everyone's surprise, they called her, together with another girl, Shokouh Mazinani, a schoolgirl. Nahid exclaimed joyously:

"I told you so! Today I'm going to see Massoud!"

And she left. They executed her the same day.

The recanting women or Kapos

In unit 246 there were a certain number of traitors and spies. By their lying reports, they made daily life even harder for us. Some had gone so far in betrayal that they were even given the job of firing the fatal shots into the heads of the executed women and didn't scruple to do whatever the executioners asked them to.

One day, those filthy creatures came to say to us: *"Put on your veils, your brothers are coming."* By this they meant the pasdaran and the bloodthirsty torturers. We didn't know why they were coming. Everyone had to stay in her place and wait. After a few minutes, the torturers came into the cell, accompanied by a woman who wore a mask over her face. She came forward and stopped just above Afkham who was sitting down. She paused, then, in silence and hidden behind her mask, like the angel of death, she looked over the girls, one by one. We could feel the icy and repulsive look of the demon of death that had spread its wings like a huge dragon over the whole room and was choosing its victims in silence.

I told myself that they were certain to be looking for someone.

Who was that black shadow who was so tall? Her corpulence didn't match anyone I knew. When she turned her face towards the girls, with that despicable mask, my heart began beating a retreat, so hard it sounded in my ears. Which girl did that deathly ghost want to send to the execution squad or to be tortured?

My head followed hers, to find out on whom her look would rest. The pasdaran checked all the rooms of the unit with that black demon and then left. The girls who had had the most experience said that she was a traitor who had come to identify all those who had not yet been identified. As a good number of girls used a nickname outside, once they were arrested they had a chance of not being tracked down. That's why they brought in traitors to recognise them. Many girls were identified in this way and then executed.

When they left, Afkham came to see me. She was very pale: *"Did you see? The danger literally passed just over my head! The traitor was Haleh. She used to work in the association of student supporters of the Mojahedin. She came to identify me, but as I was sitting just underneath her, she couldn't see my face, otherwise she'd have denounced me. In any case, you'll know that if they come for me, she'll be the one who denounced me."*

Another spy and traitor at the unit was Sedigheh. Strong, talkative and lazy, she was the one in charge, or more exactly the chief tell-tale, of our unit. She was always saying out loud: *"I'm guilty, I deserve to be executed."* By doing so she wanted to prove her devotion to the torturers and get on the prisoners' nerves. One day, a girl got up and said to her: *"Listen! They don't execute just any old piece of filth! What are you worrying about?"* Everyone laughed. She stopped talking and never repeated her idiotic remarks.

The "court"!

One day in February 1982, I was summoned to the court. As I was blindfolded, I don't remember the place exactly, but many prisoners, men and women, also with blindfolds, were in the corridor, waiting to appear.

Khomeini's court! I think that if you haven't seen the mullahs' tribunals at Evin prison, you absolutely can't imagine them or form any idea of them.

What they called the "court" was a room in Evin prison, the centre of crime. Even in appearance, there was no difference between a torture chamber and that so-called court room. It was an ordinary room with a desk and chairs placed anyhow without any order. Immediately, I was reminded of the real estate agents' offices in the neighbourhood where I grew up.

A mullah, one of those who announced the punish-ments in the torture chambers, played the part of the judge. One or two torturers accompanied him in the part of attorney. Very often, the prisoners didn't even know that they were being tried. They thought it was just one more interrogation! The prisoner or the defendant arrived with blindfolded eyes. He could see neither the judge, nor the attorney. In any case he was alone. Not only had he no bar-rister, but he had absolutely no right to defend himself, un-less he signed his own death warrant. Judgment was given in a few minutes.

In fact, it was simply a question of telling the prisoner what his sentence was. As to the judgment, it depended on the torturer's report and the judge's mood that day. If he was in good spirits, it sometimes happened that he didn't announce any death sentences. But if anything had hap-pened, for example if Khomeini had declared: *"Be merci-less!"* or if a Mojahed had spat in his face, invariably, it was a death sentence.

Thus, in principle, that court didn't try to find out where the records were, who the prisoner was or what he had done.

When I was summoned to the court, my torturers boasted of having successfully attacked a base belonging to the Mojahedin; several militants had been killed. My judges were therefore in very good spirits. This is why, that day, everyone only got prison sentences.

When my turn came, I was asked my name, my age and my civil status. I was reproached for still being single and they insisted that if I was freed, I must get married at once. I was condemned to three years in prison and went back to the unit.

The girls were very happy, especially those I knew before going to prison. They thought that the danger had passed for the moment and celebrated. A secret celebration, of course, with all the constraints of prison.

In fact, it was Tahmineh who had selflessly accepted the responsibility and took the blame for me, for us, and for many others who were never arrested. Otherwise, it was a question of sheer luck.

In the meantime, I had no news of Shekar. She wasn't at Evin. If she had been there, we should have had some news of her.

Details concerning arrests or executions reached us through the people who were going to be interrogated or tortured. That was one of their most important tasks: collecting the details and then reporting them to the unit and the other girls, transmitting them to the other units so that finally they could be passed outside.

Each prisoner obtained information from her family and also gave news from the prison to her relatives. It was an important aspect of resistance in the prison. The enemy tries to cut the prisoners off from the world and prevent them from giving news to their families in order to be able to do whatever it wants. And the prisoners had to fight that.

Sometimes we were able to find information in the newspapers. But in spite of all that, I had no news of Shekar.

The first visit

From my arrival in prison until my "trial" I was not allowed to have any visits. After my sentencing, they gave me permission and finally after three or four months I was able to see my father and mother again. But no one else. Even brothers and sisters didn't have permission to come. And even then, those visits were accompanied by blows, curses and humiliations.

Sometimes the pasdaran made the families wait for several hours in the cold or in stifling heat and finally refused to allow them to visit.

They persecuted those who protested or complained even more.

Hadj Davoud, the director of Ghezel Hessar prison, was in the habit of saying: *"Your mothers and fathers belong to the same set as you: if they were not, you would not be Hypocrites[7]."*

Thus, with that excuse, they tormented the prisoners' relatives on their visits.

In spite of all that mistreatment and humiliation, it was they, those fathers and above all those mothers, who brought us important help. In the most impossible situations, at the risk of being arrested and even executed, they helped us with all their love.

It was thanks to those visits that I learned that Shekar was in prison at Ghezel Hessar.

---

7. The derogatory name given by the regime to the Mojahedin.

An artist in our unit

Madame Mahin Bozorgi was a former artist who did dubbing for the radio. She had been arrested and found herself in our unit. She had been tortured because, at the moment of her arrest, she had on her a foreign magazine with a caricature of Khomeini. She had been condemned to ten years in prison for that. But Madame Bozorgi was old and ill; she had many health problems.

As she was an artist, she underwent many more tortures, insults and humiliations at a time. Like any other free spirit, and although she was in no way involved in politics, she was devastated by the regime's crimes.

When one day they summoned three young students to be executed, she lost control of herself. She started to cry and tremble: *"But where is God? Where is God? I no longer implore him. How can he accept those three little buds disappearing at their age? Whatever they say, you can't call children 'terrorists'. What have they done to be killed?"* She couldn't grasp the nature of those torturers. It was at that moment that I realised that Khomeini and his supporters were accusing God of their own crimes and distanced people from the faith and the Lord. I began to explain it to Madame Bozorgui: *"Be sure that the blood won't flow in vain. The innocence of those children will catch up with their executioners. That's why the torturers are condemned to disappear. That's why God exists. There are rules in this world, all the same."*

I said to her: *"Look! One day, people saw the moon reflect a picture of Khomeini. And now, what's happening? You have heard the torturers saying: 'You so and so prisoners, it's because of you that people insult Khomeini in public!' Be sure of it: these days will pass and those people will disappear too."*

When I had finished, Madame Bozorgi grew a little calmer and looked at me. *"You're right,"* she said, *"they're pushing people to the limit to make them lose hope and even faith in the good God!"*

Ghezel Hessar prison

In spite of dozens of daily executions, there was never enough room in prison, because it was excessively over-crowded. They, therefore, had to transfer those who had already been sentenced. So, during the winter of 1982, I was transferred to Ghezel Hessar.

I thought that in this new prison, the pasdaran let the prisoners serve their sentences. I still hadn't learned to know this enemy of humanity.

At Ghezel Hessar, I was transferred to the 7th sub-unit of the 3rd unit. To my knowledge, Ghezel Hessar had three units. The 1st and 3rd held political prisoners and the 2nd held the miserable Iraqi prisoners of war[8] captured by the pasdaran. We sometimes heard the volleys that executed them. When one knows what the torturers do to their own compatriots, one no longer doubts what they are capable of doing to foreign prisoners. Very often I felt pity for those prisoners.

Once through the door, there was a wide corridor where the prison warders were established. Another long corridor continued it with, on the left, the "solitary" units and, on the right, collective units. Then there was the visiting room corridor. It is possible that these descriptions are not very precise because I was blindfolded. There may therefore have been other rooms which I couldn't see.

---

8. Iran-Iraq war from 1980 to 1988.

First they put each prisoner in a "solitary" cell. Then, after an enquiry that lasted from a few days to a week, the time necessary to "know" her, they put her in a collective unit.

Sub-unit 6 was for men, 7 for women and 8 the disciplinary cell. Sub-units 3 and 4 were women's collectives. I don't know whether the men's collective unit was in that block or not.

I was sent into 7. Once through the metal entrance grille, you went into a square passage with a big room on each side. No doubt those were the rest or work rooms of the unit's warders. Those rooms were separated from the central passage by grilles. Then came the entrance to the sub-unit, also with metal bars. On each side, there were six cells: the size of an army bed, they were no more than 50 centimetres wide.

Each cell contained three bunk beds and a window measuring 50 to 60 centimetres. Closed by bars, this window gave onto the sub-unit's exercise area in the left-hand cells, and onto that of no. 7, where we were, for the right-hand ones. The cells were numbered 1 to 6 on the left and 7 to 12 on the right. The lavatories were between cells 3 and 4 on the left and the shower between cells 7 and 8 on the right. The entrance to the exercise yard was situated after the 12th cell.

At first sight, each cell seemed intended to contain three people, but on entering, I noticed about fifteen people in each cell. That means that instead of thirty-six, there were nearly two hundred prisoners in the sub-unit.

The members of the other political groups, twenty-five to thirty people, were assembled in a room by the entrance. They were called *"the non-religious"*[9] prisoners. Among them, there were militant members of the Toudeh party and the Aksariat party, two organisations which had allied themselves with those in power and accused us of being responsible for the regime's crimes! They didn't hesitate to juxtapose the roles of torturer and victim. That was the culmination of their betrayal.

But in prison, we tried not to stir up our differences with those militants and, faced with the regime, we drew them towards us so that those in power couldn't take advantage of that conflict.

Because of the terrible overcrowding, the lock-up doors were left open and the girls were outside the cells, that is to say in the whole space of the sub-unit. Each one had her place to sleep. There too we were squashed like sardines, but at least we didn't have to take turns in sleeping. So that those whose place was in front of the lavatories, the showers or the places where people had to pass weren't always the same ones, and that they all had the chance to rest, we had a weekly rota. The beds in the cells were reserved for the mothers, the children and the invalids.

If the enemy evaluated us on our arrival, we in our turn evaluated him. At once, I tried to identify the spies. The person in charge of the unit was a traitor called Sima. She was pale, with a broad forehead, colourless eyes and swollen eyelids. At a distance, you might have thought she had a line in the place of her eyes. She wore a pair of glasses and, with her expressionless face, she looked like a mem-

---

9. The prison authorities and the revolutionary guards divided the political prisoners into two categories: the People's Mojahedin whom they dubbed Hypocrites, and the entirety of members and supporters of the Marxist groups, all tendencies lumped together, whom they called the "unbelievers" or "non-religious" prisoners.

ber of the Gestapo as depicted in films. So "*Gestapo*" was
what we called her. Everyone called her that. She was the
torturer Hadj Davoud's chief sneak.

There were also two other women, whom one could
immediately liken to pasdaran. The same cold, soulless
look, full of hatred. It was strange that those who took
Khomeini's side became exactly like him and were easily
recognisable.

As soon as I arrived in the unit, Mansoureh Fatahian,
whom I knew from university and had seen at the association and during various activities, came joyfully up to me.
I too was very happy to see her. It seems odd that one can
be pleased to see a friend or an acquaintance in prison, because logically it ought to be the opposite. But under Khomeini's regime, that was logical or at least comprehensible
because in fact, you're glad to see the person still alive and
that trumps your regret at seeing her imprisoned.

Mansoureh briefed me as much as was necessary on
the situation and the organisation of the unit, as well as on
the prisoners. I also knew one or two "non religious" girls
who were in Evin. They had been transferred to Ghezel
Hessar before me. I was on better terms with one of them,
because not only did I know her from Evin, but she was a
nurse. We therefore agreed to make use of this connection
to coordinate our actions with their group, particularly in
order to exchange information.

At Ghezel, as at Evin, nobody asked questions about
anyone's background, because not only was it useless, but
it added to the danger.

That first day, I was sitting beside Mansoureh when
Gestapo came up and said to me: "*You who are a nurse, take
responsibility for the unit's pharmacy, because the other one's*

gone into a collective unit." I thought at first that this would be an act of collaboration with the regime and refused. But Mansoureh signalled me to accept and I did so. All the girls were pleased: *"That's good, because if you hadn't accepted, they would have put in one of their own people who wouldn't have done anything for the patients. Besides, you can go to the infirmary and bring back news."*

The guards never opened the door of the yard which was under our unit and sub-unit 8. Thus, we had nowhere to walk and the girls left their linen to dry in the cells. With a great deal of ingenuity, they had organised their life in that tiny space that contained 15 people. Thus, they had hammered nails into the wall near the ceiling, and stretched a rope for drying linen. The ropes and the bags for wet linen were woven out of plastic bags. They had also made dressing-cases, sock-bags and a whole heap of other things out of old clothes. And all that was hung on the wall so as not to clutter up the cell. But as the girls were deprived of exercise and sunlight and lived side by side squashed like sardines, skin diseases proliferated. The girls did try to keep the invalids' belongings separate, but given the overcrowding, it was practically impossible.

The day after my arrival we were told that the doctor was coming to see the patients. He came to the unit once a week. As I had medical responsibility for the unit, I should normally have been present at his consultations. Doctor A. had worked in the Shah's palace, and now he was in prison, he worked for the regime. He had recanted.

"Are you the nurse who's just arrived?" he asked when he saw me.

"Yes!"

"Are you prepared to come to the infirmary to work?"

"No!" I retorted like lightning, looking offended.

And that's what he reported to Hadj Davoud Rahmani. The girls were disappointed in my answer, because it would have been a very good opportunity to infiltrate their system and communicate with the other parts of the prison. The most tenacious of us worked in the infirmary, but I didn't know that.

Part Four

Ghezel Hessar prison

A savage gorilla

Hadj Davoud Rahmani, the director of Gezel Hessar prison, was a truly repulsive yob. That scrap-iron merchant had become one of the pasdaran after Khomeini's arrival, then a prison warder and torturer. As his bosses had been satisfied with the way he tortured Mojahedin resisters, they had entrusted the direction of Ghezel Hessar prison to him. He was mercilessly cruel, and as stupid as he was backward.

He classified people in his mind. Then he tortured and maltreated them according to that classification. For instance, he hated those who wore glasses; he said that they were theoreticians.

Similarly, he believed that tall people were the Mojahedin's bodyguards and he felt a bestial hatred for them. As to students, the very word made him hysterical. He execrated blue-eyed people; he had a religious saying about that. All kinds of people, one way or another, found themselves on his black list and fell under the blows of his violence and torture. Every time he came to the unit, with or without a pretext, he verbally abused everyone. Then he took a few girls away with him, beat them and insulted them before sending them back.

One day, some girls whistled a song of the resistance: a father's last kiss to his daughter, before her execution. They didn't realise that it was forbidden. Suddenly the door opened and Gestapo came in, panicking.

"Ladies, ladies!" she howled, *"put your veils on! Hadj Agha[1] wants to come in!"*

Everyone rushed for a veil in order to hide from those yobs' lubricious looks.

Hadj Agha and his favourite pasdar, Ahmad, came in. We were all sitting down. He stayed at the entrance to the unit and opened his disgusting mouth to spit out what he himself deserved:

"So what's going on? You're whistling for the men who are on the other side of the wall? That means: 'Come and kiss me'? The brothers who have recanted have come to let you know. Bitches! But where did they pick you up when they brought you here? Luckily this wall's able to hold you in, we know very well what you'd do otherwise!"

The girls knew that the best way to make that torturer look ridiculous was to keep quiet.

That's why we did nothing but look at him. As to myself, I was knitting coloured threads taken from my socks with two safety-pins which I had pulled out to form needles. And in my heart, I replied to his insults. I knew that he very much wanted someone to answer so as to be able to vent his hatred. By our silence we were forcing him to either to take everyone to be punished, or no one. And he didn't want that. When I was almost certain that nobody was going to answer, two girls, non-religious ones, stood

---

1. Hadj Davoud.

up:

"Hadj Agha, it's not true, we're not like that," they exclaimed.

As if he didn't know it! We suddenly had the impression that he had reached his goal, his hunger was satisfied. He grew calm.

"Good! ...The gossips have been identified ... Outside! Get out!" You'll be back soon," he added with a sly smile.

And the warders took them away. We knew from experience that after having hit them at the entrance, they would transfer them to sub-unit 8 which was reserved for punishment. That's what they did. They came back two weeks later. They had unfortunately joined those who had recanted.

In this way, Hadj Davoud tried to track down the weakest ones, separate them from the group and make them crack as fast as possible under torture, then send them back to the unit as his trump cards, to frighten the others and show them that all resistance was useless. But as he said himself, with the Mojahedin, that trick didn't have much chance of working.

Various aspects of collective resistance

Once, not long before dawn, everyone was asleep, and at that moment I was placed near the entrance of the unit. Suddenly, there came a noise from behind the door. I pricked up my ears; it was Hadj Davoud speaking to Gestapo. I listened carefully. He was asking her for an account and giving her directions:

"You stupid bitch! I've told you a thousand times that I don't give a damn if the lefties are doing crosswords or read-

ing newspapers. We know them! Find the Hypocrites' network. Cretin! You haven't bothered to bring me a single report on their activities. Does that mean they're doing nothing? But who fobbed me off with a fool like you! If you go one being so useless, I'll throw you where you deserve to be."

That meant more pressure on the girls, even more constraints, and the disappearance of the few resources we had. This information was transmitted to everyone. That was the *"network"* Hadji[2] was looking for. A very rudimentary network, no doubt, but it was the only way the prisoners had to protect themselves from a regime which had the leisure to do absolutely anything it wanted.

The result of this collective communication was the coordinated movement of the prisoners, as well as a system of collecting and distributing information. This maddened Hadji and the other pasdaran. That's how resistance continued to exist in prison.

At Ghezel Hessar were kept those who had been longest in prison, those who had been arrested on 20 June 1981 or earlier. So, Shekar was there too. But the girls said she was in sub-unit 8. I tried very hard to see her, without success.

I don't know through what outside pressure or through what calculation it was finally possible to take some exercise. Everyone had the right to that except for sub-unit 8 who were being punished.

The windows of the cells of sub-unit 8 also gave onto that exercise yard. The first day, I saw Shekar and she called to me. My God! Shekar! My sweet, gentle friend! When I saw her, I felt myself growing wings, I wanted so much,

---

2. Hadj Davoud.

just once, to press her in my arms.

In the fraction of a second, pictures of the past came back to my mind. If only I could, as when we were students, tangle her carefully combed hair, or snatch the remains of her sandwich to eat it under her astonished eyes, so that she could then smile at me, shaking her head. I should have loved to relive that time when my father teased Shekar because of her first name (which means "powdered sugar") and she laughed so much that she cried. How she laughed!

Sometimes people's wishes and hopes can be so simple and yet seem so inaccessible ...

Now, the Shekar I adored was two or three metres away from me, up there behind the bars. But I couldn't even look her in the face. I tried to communicate with her while I was walking and looking in other directions. Shekar did the same. However, thanks to the girls' help and watchfulness, I was able to talk to her and tell her all I wanted to.

The prisoners of sub-unit 8 experienced conditions even harder than ours, because at least thirty people were piled up in each cell and their doors were shut. Later we were told that in order to bolt them, they gave the girls kicks. The prisoners then remained upright or hung on to the beds of the cell. It was for this reason that Shekar was always at the window. She had found room for herself, crouched on the window sill.

Those were really inhumane conditions. Once every twenty-four hours, the prisoners had three minutes to go to the lavatories. In that oppressive and insufferable climate, it was impossible to hold out. They were forced to relieve themselves in a bucket or a plastic bag which they could only empty when the door was opened. I can't imagine how they managed to do it, squashed to the greatest possible extent, without even being able to move.

The weakest ones and the invalids were suffocating because of the lack of oxygen and the congestion. They lost consciousness. Keeping someone conscious in that situation and fighting to keep her alive is extremely difficult.

Hadj Davoud, the torturer, came every day to persecute them more. He said with his yobbish insulting air: *"Resist! Resist! Until the 'heroic people*[3] *come to your help!"* Or else: *"So where's your dear Massoud*[4] *who's supposed to be coming to help you? You Hypocrite bastards, we'll keep you here so long that your hair will be as white as your teeth and your teeth will be as black as your hair!"*

Shekar too was in one of those cells. But her face showed only serenity, which was exactly what put Hadji beside himself. Shekar said: *"We are shut in,"* but I didn't understand what she meant.

Later on the girls explained that this meant that the cell doors were shut. It was one of the prison expressions and one of that torturer's most frequent tortures. However, two days later, I no longer saw Shekar at the window. The frame was empty. Looking for her, I learned that because of their resistance, they had been transferred to the isolation cells of Gohardasht prison to be tortured even more.

Tea in the bath!

The rule about bathing was the same as at Evin. But the bathroom was smaller and had only three shower cabinets. Three people had to go into each cabinet in a quarter of

---

3. An allusion to the Mojahedin's expression meaning the Iranian people.

4. An allusion to Massoud Rajavi, Leader of the Iranian Resistance.

an hour. Every week, the responsibility for the shower was entrusted to a different prisoner. She had to plan and regulate each person's order and time under the shower. She also had to tell each one how much time she had left. The programme was drawn up in advance and the first row was always ready to go straight under the shower. Another prisoner was delegated to watch how much time for hot water was left and announce immediately the moment the temperature was at its highest so as to make tea with that water. It was very funny and we called it "the tea in the bath". We had kept some metal cans that we had washed. When the water was hot, the tea team took hold of the cans and prepared the tea at top speed; then they wrapped the cans in blankets to keep them warm. When the two hours for bathing were over, we shared out that tea which was tepid and colourless, but with no bromide. We took such pleasure in it that we felt we were drinking the best tea in the world.

Normally, in the morning, we were given a pan of water with a lot of bromide. The one who was on duty, and whom we called the worker for the day, prepared the tea and gave everyone half a glass. This tea was something which the girls had got used to and for which they felt a continual need.

If nothing special happened, we had the right to half an hour's exercise. If the pasdaran made us go out at any time other than the one for exercise, it meant that there was going to be a search, that our things would be disarranged and that they would take some girls away... or else, that a new one was coming. It was better in fact to bring in a new prisoner when the others were away, so that they couldn't let her know about the spies' and wardresses' tricks. And besides, in that case, the pasdaran had time to size her up. The girls from the provinces, who didn't know that stratagem, let themselves be taken in.

They let themselves be conned by the spies, told them everything they shouldn't have and caused problems for everyone, themselves included. One afternoon, we were sent out of the unit and we understood that new ones would be brought in. We tried to get in on various pretexts, but it was impossible. After having discussed it, I was designated to go.

"One of the girls is feeling ill, I must get some medicaments," I said, knocking on the door.

It worked. Gestapo opened it.

"What's going on, madam?" she asked with her unpleasant voice and icy look.

"The girls have been out of doors for a long time and they're cold. The one with asthma isn't well. She's having an attack."

I talked loudly and took the opportunity to check everything, especially to observe the newcomers. There were two women, one of them with a little girl ten months old. We learned later on that they were Maryam and Ategheh, with a daughter Atiyeh. Taking advantage of the situation and on the pretext of kissing the child, I went up to them. Leaning towards the little girl, I said to them softly: *"Don't say anything! They're spies!"* and took the child in my arms. I went to part of the cell where the medicaments were kept. But it was too late. The newcomers had spoken at length about the resistance of the girls of Babol, and of the pasdaran's crimes in that town, and had said that Babol was like fire beneath ashes. They had also given details about them. That would certainly cost them dear. Hadji, coming next day to put pressure on, asked: *"So the new Hypocrites have arrived? And so Babol's like fire beneath ashes, eh?"* It was a direct threat against Maryam and Ategheh.

The little thinker's secret

A few days later, a little boy and his mother, Akhtar, who was a supporter of the Fedayin, were transferred to sub-unit 7. He was called Rouzbeh and was three or four years old. Taking into account the restrictions and lack of resources, the presence of children in prison was, physically and psychologically, extremely difficult. Their destiny made everyone suffer. But they brought a breath of the joy of living into those cellars of death and horror.

The *"aunties"* adored those children and took them under their wings to nurture them. They sewed fine clothes for them and decorated them with flowers. They offered them pretty fabric dolls, with woven hair, fabric balls or other toys made entirely from recycled old clothes. The most astonishing thing was that, on their side, the children too recognised the *"aunties"* and didn't confuse them with the spies. And they even defended them with courage.

Little Atiyeh started dancing as soon as she heard any music. She stretched out her little arms on each side of her body and twirled her wrists. She swung her head to right and left and performed a very pretty dance. The girls liked her way of dancing so much that they took her in their arms and murmured a song in her ears. Then she automatically began to dance, which made us all laugh ... and everyone wanted to take her in her arms.

As to Rouzbeh, in spite of his young age, his behaviour wasn't in the least childlike. A deep, sad and pensive expression sprang from his large eyes. Although he didn't reject toys, none of them amused him. The "aunties" suggested all kinds of games to him, but he didn't want to play. He preferred to stay by himself and meditate. Most of the time, the girls didn't want to disturb his peace, but they still tried to divert him.

One day, when we were in the exercise yard, I saw him wearing a checked shirt and trousers with braces. He seemed so fragile. He was sitting down, leaning against the wall, his hands on his knees. His eyes were fixed on the high brick wall facing him. He wasn't paying any attention to what was happening around him.

I watched him for quite some time. He didn't even blink. I sat down gently beside him.

"Hello, Rouzbeh!"

"Hello," he answered without even raising his eyes.

"What are you thinking about, Rouzbeh?" I asked him, taking great care not to disturb him.

"I'm thinking," he said to me in a soft, sad voice, not knowing very well how to pronounce the words. *"I'm thinking that when I'm grown up, I'll be an architect and I'll pull down that wall to let you all out of there!"*

Heavens, how I wanted to cry! I hugged him in my arms, I kissed him and said: *"You'll certainly become an architect and you'll do it, and all your 'aunties' will wait for you."*

As soon as fatigue and sleep appeared on his face, he always took shelter in his mother's arms and fell asleep there. She leaned her face on the child's forehead and gently rocked him until he fell asleep. Several times I heard the same dialogue between the mother and child. She answered with one or two short sentences that didn't really provide an answer.

"Mummy!"

"Yes, my darling!"

"Where's Daddy?"

"I don't know, my boy!"

"Mummy!"

"Yes!"

"Why was Daddy like that?"

"I don't know, son. Go to sleep!"

She calmed him and put him to sleep.

One day, I asked Akhtar the reason for that invariable dialogue because I wanted to understand Rouzbeh's secret. I wanted all of us to share his great sorrow. He was far too young to endure this sadness.

"Akhtar, please, if you can, answer me. What happened to Rouzbeh's father? Why does he keep on asking you the same questions?"

Akhtar looked at me with sorrow and love. I felt from her expression that she, too, wanted her sorrow to be shared.

"When the pasdaran attacked our house," she said with a sad smile, *"they took us all away to prison. That day, they left Rouzbeh in the torture chamber beside his father. He was present at all the tortures and finally at the death of his father. In spite of his young age, he's kept the memory of those events remarkably and sees them again all the time. That's why I'm trying to make him forget them. But he keeps on asking me."*

Rouzbeh's story and that of all the other Rouzbehs are alike. How cruel and criminal is that enemy of humanity, that thief of the trust of the oppressed people of Iran! It reminded me of the story of Ategheh's children. She had told me that pasdaran had torn her husband, the engineer

Rahman Ali Abadian, to shreds under torture before shooting him. Then they had loaded the body, soaked in blood, on to the back of an uncovered wagon and had made his two sons, Mohammad and Morteza, climb into it. The little boys were not yet old enough to go to school. They made them sit down beside the deformed corpse of their father and made them go around the streets of Babol. That monster wanted, with that hideous spectacle, to display his authority and terrify the town.

Little Morteza and Mohammad bear, like Rouzbeh, the weight of devastating sorrow. With this difference, that they have to bear their misfortune alone, without their mother.

A little sparrow puts the Beast to flight!

One day, the gorilla Hadj Davoud came into the unit, howling and roaring as usual. We were all waiting to see whom he would have it in for. Those who were entitled to whipping rations were holding themselves ready. But this time, he didn't go towards them. He quickly went up to Ategheh who was carrying Atiyeh in her arms and had wrapped her in her veil. Ategheh understood and stood up, as if her maternal instinct had smelt the danger which was threatening her child. She pressed her harder against her chest.

Hadj Davoud, who because of his corpulence really did look like a gorilla, caught the little girl by the neck with his abominable paws.

"You make Hypocrites' children dance to the songs of Ahangaran[5]?! Why doesn't she dance to the songs of the organisa-

---

5. The regime's official singer.

tion?! When I've corrected her, she'll never dance again!"*

We had all stood up and were looking at Hadji with as much hatred as astonishment. Had we heard properly? Did this fool of a torturer want to punish a child ten months old? We knew that it was so as to make her mother crack.

Suddenly, Ategheh sprang up with all the strength and power of a mother who knows her child is in danger, with a swift movement, she snatched Atiyeh from the monster's claws.

"You filth!" she shouted with all her force. *"What do you want? You've tortured and killed her father, you've put us in prison. Now you want to torture a child ten months old? Be damned to you all! You filth! But what do you take us for, you and the bitches who reported to you? If you touch my daughter, you'll do it over my dead body!"*

Ategheh had taken a deep breath and insulted them all in one go. Hadji saw that the situation was too much for him, that everyone was standing up, that everyone's eyes were levelled at him with hatred and that he was on the point of losing control of the unit. So he didn't want to lose face. He sprayed us with curses and turned to Ategheh.

It was then that little Rouzbeh, who until then was at his mother's side, jumped in front of her. He barely came up to her knees. He opened his arms to protect her. His face didn't show the slightest trace of fear. There was only hatred and power. It was the strangest look I have ever seen. I don't know what was special about it, but one felt that it was the most violent attack with which the torturer was confronted and that it floored him. It was as if, in that silent look, the child was sending back to him everything Ategheh had shouted at him to defend her daughter. It was as if his eyes were sending back all his father's shrieks under torture. Hadji couldn't stand it.

Without meaning to, he lowered his voice, admitting his powerlessness and his defeat.

"Now you put children in front of us so as to stop us taking action? You'll see!" he threatened, beating retreat.

The recanting women and the spies, feeling scorched, had fled to their room; they shut the door and stayed in their hole for quite a time.

That's how I saw with my own eyes how powerful a mother's and a child's love could be and how they could overpower a savage. But we knew that this victory wouldn't be without reprisals.

Zohreh's story

Zohreh Chavoshi was a girl who, it appears, had been arrested because she worked in the office of Bani Sadr or in one of his organisations. But when she had known the Mojahedin in prison, she had become a supporter of that movement. Her brother-in-law and quite a few of her near relations formed part of Hezbollah and the pasdaran.

As there were no definite grounds of accusation against her and Bani Sadr had been the president of the regime, the fact of working under him could not constitute a fault. She hadn't been freed, however. In fact, she resisted the torturers, opposed their actions against the prisoners and defied Hadji.

Her relations did everything to get her out, but as Hadji couldn't force her to collaborate or recant, he didn't know what to do with her. He told her she was *"worse than the hypocrites,"* and that otherwise he would have set her free.

Zohreh, who was a hardworking girl from the southern suburbs, wouldn't agree to submit to such stupid mercenaries as Hadji.

She was weak and ill. She had a stomach problem and couldn't swallow the prison food. Most of her meals consisted of dry bread and cheese. We had no extra cheese, but we put a little aside for the invalids and shared out the rest.

Because of her illness and malnutrition, Zohreh had become very thin and fragile; she barely weighed 40 kg. In spite of everything, she stood up to Hadji, and that was admirable. She was very much loved and respected. She was always there to support the Mojahedin in difficulties, whoever the enemy was. She never gave in. She was killed after being set free from prison, when trying to rejoin the Mojahedin.

Permanent persecutions and tortures

Every day the torturers invented new forms of persecution to break the prisoners and, as for us, we did everything we could to resist.

The nights were cold and the prison heating sent asphyxiating smoke into the unit. We insisted that the warders should turn it off, but in vain. We then had to leave the windows open to avoid being suffocated. The untreated asthmatics were sometimes at death's door. The unit's floor, which was made of mosaic, was covered with carpeting full of holes, as thin as cloth.

As the floor was icy, we had spread out blankets on it; those that remained were shared. We had organised teams in order to share out the blankets. We spread the army blankets on the floor and covered ourselves with good blankets sent by some of our families; otherwise the intolerable cold would have prevented us from closing our eyes.

One night when we were asleep, the torturers intruded into our unit. Each one of us had to take up a blanket and go out. Nobody knew what it was about and where they wanted to take us. We all went out. We were told to face the wall. They hit us and insulted us. The recanting women, who were mainly responsible for this incident, came and went like scared hyenas, showing their zeal to the torturers.

After having kept us waiting in the cold, Hadj Davoud finally arrived. He opened his dirty mouth again to cover us in obscenities:

"I've heard it said that you're sharing blankets and doing filthy things underneath. You're in the Islamic Republic's university here!"

And he spewed out the ton of enormities that he was in the habit of bawling.

What an obsessive! He had already admitted it once. One day when he had made the sisters leave the unit in order to punish them, he had thrown them to the ground with blows from a whip and ordered them to crawl from one end of the unit to the other. Then he had said to one of his fellows: *"Look! We used to run after so many women and now they're at our feet."*

They kept us in the yard, in the cold, until the small hours. They took all our blankets away. They only left us one each (the one that the family had brought, or an army blanket).

As soon as we went back to the unit, we immediately reorganised. First, to annoy the recanting women, we had a good laugh. Then we declared that tonight we would sleep with all our things. *"All our things"* has a particular meaning in prison. When we said that so and so had been taken away with all her things or that the warders were calling a prisoner and specifying *"that she should bring all her things,"* it meant that we shouldn't see her again. She was leaving to be executed or for another fate.

The spies didn't understand what it was about. When evening came, we very gently reminded all the girls: *"All your things!"* Everyone went to fetch them and everyone got dressed in everything she owned. We gave clothes to those who didn't have enough of them. Everyone was wearing three or four pairs of socks on top of one another, and two or three scarves.

In short, we had put on everything we had. Our disguise made us laugh, it amused us a lot. Then, divided into teams of four or five, we spread the blankets on the ground, as the floor was really cold! We stretched ourselves out and covered ourselves with our veils and sheets. Only the invalids were allowed a blanket. In this way, we answered the regime and its spies back and conquered the cold. It warmed us to see the discouragement and agitation on the faces of the recanting women.

Everything's forbidden!

At Ghezel, the girls made art objects with very rudimentary means. For example, they created very pretty statuettes and little flowers which they painted with the ink from fountain pens. They then arranged them in toothbrush cases, as if in passe-partout mountings. They also sewed very fine pieces by unravelling knitwear or worn-out socks. They used unfolded safety-pins as knitting needles. They also made pretty things out of pebbles and date stones which they then offered, when it was possible, to their children or their visiting families.

But as it was a kind of resistance which kept up the prisoners' spirits, the regime forbade so as to increase the pressure. First the warders gathered up the newspapers and books, then religious books and finally the Qur'an. Either they found a pretext to justify these bans, or they squarely made us responsible. Thus they suppressed the page of the newspaper devoted to crosswords, because the girls did them together and it was therefore a *"collective act."* Then they judged that the text of the articles was the starting point for political analyses and forbade newspapers. Their own newspapers! Then they confiscated the religious books. *"You're organised and you read them to use them against us."*

There only remained the Qur'an. It seemed hard to justify forbidding that. By making such a decision, it was as if the regime, which called itself Islamic and claimed to have brought us to *"university"* to give us a religious formation, was spitting on itself. But that didn't stop Khomeini's men. They didn't even look for justification. A little later, they forbade plastic art. They could forbid and confiscate everything, but they couldn't touch the prisoners' hearts.

When the regime used the crosswords as an excuse to suppress the newspapers, Manijeh said: *"Never mind! They want to demoralise us, we'll show them."* That very evening, she had made an even bigger and more elaborate crossword grid than the one in the newspaper with more amusing subjects. From that day on, compiling crosswords became one of her main occupations. She worked at it without ceasing and they were really of very high quality.

During walks I often saw a girl who, sitting down, was rubbing a stone against the wall. Two other prisoners kept watch. If a spy approached, they warned the girl with a word or a noise agreed in advance. And this stratagem made it possible, after a few days, to create a beautiful stone object.

The girls went on producing objects in secret, helping one another and not letting the regime get the better of them. They kept finding means of continuing the fight.

Thus, faced with the regime's technique for increasing repression, the girls found a way of neutralising it. But they paid a high price for it under torture or in the punishment block.

Boycott and punishment of the recanting women

The girls had their own way of standing up to the recanting women and the spies, and neutralising them. First of all, nobody ate with them. When one of them sat down beside a girl, she got up and changed places. Nobody spoke to them or greeted them. When they asked us questions, we only answered yes or no. We never let slip an occasion to mock them.

Once, the warders deprived us of exercise for a few days. Nahid and Azar, two schoolgirls overflowing with energy, adored getting up practical jokes against the traitors. Seeing Gestapo come into the unit, Azar shouted: *"Go on, girls! The yard's open."* All of a sudden, so as to be first and because the clothes had been outside for several days, the girls rushed towards the door, towards Gestapo... They practically crushed her. Dying of fright, she managed to wrench herself free, her hair in a mess and her glasses crooked. She ran like mad towards the entrance. When the girls saw that the yard was shut, they came back, groaning.

Gestapo came back when she had regained her self-control.

"Madame, why did you say: 'The yard's open'?" she asked Azar in an inquisitorial tone.

"What?! Me?! I never said a thing like that. I only asked: 'Girls ... the yard's open?'"

And we heard more bursts of laughter. You should have seen Gestapo's face!

Another time, the torturer Lajevardi came into our unit, accompanied by the mullahs Moussavi Ardebili and Hadi Khameneï and a few other torturers.

Because of the small number of recanting women, they had brought pasdaran and recanting women from other units to shout slogans on their arrival, because as for us, we never repeated their nonsense. When they arrived, those women who were sold out, started howling: *"Blessed be Muhammad, here is the smell of Beheshti[6]."*

"Hey, girls, it stinks! It's killing us! Shut the shithouse door!" retorted Nahid.

We found it very hard not to burst out laughing. The recanting women didn't dare denounce us for that, and besides, they didn't know who had spoken.

Manijeh Shakeri was a schoolgirl of 15, full of mischief and the joy of living. She had very interesting techniques for mocking the spies. She had nicknamed one traitor *"the witch"*. In fact, the latter wore spectacles on the end of an interminable nose, which, it's true, really made her look

---

6. Ayatollah Beheshti was at the head of the judicial power and the second most important personage in the regime after Khomeini.

like a witch. Not an evening passed without Manijeh play-ing a trick on her. For quite a time, when the witch woke up, she found herself with a broom beside her head. Then Manijeh said: *"I parked her vehicle above her head,"* which made everyone laugh. But the witch didn't understand, un-til one day she realised that she was the witch. She went to complain to Hadji: *"The Hypocrites call me a witch."* All the cells nearly burst with laughing. She begged him to take her out of the unit. Finally she was transferred.

Obligatory instruction

At Ghezel, just as at Evin, on some days there were obliga-tory "instruction sessions". Mullahs, or people who claimed to be such, came to "counsel" us. They took us out of the units by force to make us sit in the corridor opposite. Then they unpacked their obscenities. Several evenings running, a young mullah tried to make us participate in his sessions. In the end he was begging us. I think that if he had succeed-ed in making us play out his scenario, he would have been rewarded. But as he had achieved nothing, he apologised and even implored us. Then he started insulting us as our tormentors did when torturing us. Then we understood that he was a torturer playing the part of a *"teacher"*...

Hadji noticed the failure of his project: making the prisoners recant... Breaking their resistance was impossi-ble. He contorted himself like a wounded snake. He wan-dered about with his huge carcass and howled torrents of insults like a madman. When he passed by us, when we had got up to return to the unit, he violently struck a girl whose head hit the wall with brutal force. She fell to the ground, senseless. We picked her up and brought her back to the unit in a coma. A haematoma had formed on her forehead at the place of the blow,. We insisted on her being taken to the infirmary, but the warders wouldn't agree. We watched over her all night, putting compresses of fresh water on her forehead, because she was in danger of a contusion on the brain. She regained consciousness two or three hours later, but we preferred to keep her under observation for twenty-four hours. Happily, all was well.

These criminals knew no bounds. Khomeini had given them a free hand. He had reassured them with a fatwa: *"The lives, the possessions and the relations of the Hypocrites have no value and no one will be held responsible if they die under torture."*

We knew it very well and that's why we contrived to act collectively and not alone, so as not to be tracked down. Because, faced with a group, our torturers found things more difficult. Even with collective initiatives and actions, we couldn't act openly.

When the regime really wanted to stop us acting, it pestered the others. If one of us decided not to go to those educational sessions, not only was she tortured, but all her cellmates were punished too. The girls dreaded that, because they didn't want someone else to be tortured through their fault.

Part Five

The Cage

From March 1983 onwards, a certain number of resisting women, including Shekar, were taken to Gohardasht to suffer further tortures. They were forbidden to have visits. Their families didn't know where they were and wandered from prison to prison in search of them. We learned afterwards that they had been transferred to special places for torture, unknown to everyone, later called *"the habitable units"*.

They were located at Ghezel Hessar prison. Apparently they were units that had formerly been used by the prison staff, or disused offices.

After having been interrogated and tortured again in the disciplinary blocks at Evin, these prisoners were sent to the first unit of Ghezel Hessar, nicknamed *"the cages"*. Until then everyone was ignorant of the existence of *"the last judgment unit"*, *"the cages"* and the *"habitable units"*. Even in Ghezel, we didn't know they existed. We only knew that there were places for punishment in the first unit and that men had been taken there, without any more details.

Until, one evening in 1982, the warders made us leave our units to make us undergo an *"educational programme"*. We were expecting the arrival of a mullah – or rather an ersatz mullah – to make us another speech. Suddenly, we were surprised to see a few *"unbelieving prisoners"* arrive. They had been taken out of the unit a week earlier because they didn't pray. We didn't know where they had been transferred.

They were there in front of us crying, declaring at the microphone that they had *"faith in Islam from now on,"* that they regretted having acted sinfully against that *"dear Islam"* and against the *"kind Hadji."* They asked forgiveness. They assured us that they felt no bitterness towards Islam, the mullahs and the pasdaran who had executed their close relatives. *"They did nothing except squeeze the trigger! That doesn't count! The real criminals were the United States, Israel, China, Russia and a few other countries!!!"*

The transfer to the cage

That evening, we went back to the unit with a bitter feeling. We knew that this "victory" of the regime would have grave consequences for each of us. The very next day, the spies became strangely aggressive; they pestered the girls for no reason at all. We absolutely refused to answer. That day, the water in the shower was hot and as usual, we had taken some water to make tea. Suddenly they called about fifteen people, including Azam, Sarah, Djamileh, and a few others whose names I've forgotten, to make them leave the unit. The situation was explosive.

Tavous, a recanting woman, came towards me. *"Good,"* she snapped nastily, *"all you had to do was not make tea collectively!"* Those dishonoured people had taken those few buckets of water from the shower as a pretext for putting girls under torture. I didn't keep her waiting for an answer:

"*Shut up! I'll give you something to make you spit blood! Stop it! Bootlicker! Slut!*" I felt better, relieved, light-hearted. She left and a few moments later, I was called too. I was happy, because I didn't want to stay when my friends had been taken away.

The girls were looking at me anxiously and helping me so that I shouldn't forget any of my clothes, because it was cold. I put on all my things, knowing that coming back was out of the question. Ategheh, Maryam and others, silent and full of anxiety, escorted me with tears in their eyes. I thought how sweet little Atiyeh was and how I was going to miss her. They took me to the entrance, blindfolded me, and put me facing the wall with the others. Hadji was there and there was noise. A little later, we heard him say: "*So those are the Hypocrites in chief? Very good. They're going to a place they won't come out of until they're corrected, or they're dead. Super! My machine for making women recant is fascinating!*" And he spewed out his usual idiocies.

We went towards the exit and climbed into a car from which we got down after a short distance. We went into another building that resembled the first and was in fact unit n° 1. The warders then kept us standing for I don't know how many hours, separated and facing the wall. Finally Hadji arrived. I had put on a thick woollen waistcoat that my aunt had knitted. When he passed in front of me he asked: "*Who's that one?*" before adding: "*Look what a strapping girl she is!*" And he hit me violently on the head with an enormous cable which he had in his hand. I felt my head spinning, but I tried not to fall and not to show my weakness. While I was trying to find out what could have hit me so hard, a rain of blows fell on me without giving me time to think. I had been stunned and my head was hurting me cruelly. I unconsciously protected my face. I knew that those blows could disfigure me. When moans escaped me, the torturer Hadj Davoud stopped. *"Take her away!"* he snapped in a whisper.

They made me turn round several times on my own axis so that I shouldn't know where I was going. But I counted the turns and I knew where I was. It's very important for a prisoner not to lose her bearings, either in time or space. One must keep an idea of the place and time. Nobody had taught me that, but, from experience and a little from instinct as well, I realised all the importance of it.

They took me to the right under the entrance door and left me in an empty room. I don't know how long afterwards they came to fetch me and we went towards the corridor and the sub-units. At the entrance to the corridor, I must have gone into a room where a woman took me in hand. She made me sit down in a space between two upright boards 50 cm apart. It was hot and heavy, it smelt like a bathroom. I still had the blindfold over my eyes. She passed her hand over my head; haematomas several centimetres thick had formed where the cable had hit me. There were also some scratches so thick that one could feel them through the headscarf and veil. It didn't hurt, it was probably numbed. I thought about the others: had they gone? What had happened to them?

In that unbreathable atmosphere, I felt myself going. I felt faint and lost consciousness. I don't know if they took me somewhere else, but I remember having been put in the middle of that big room. On my right, there was a bathroom with a hot shower or perhaps just a tap, where that woman was washing things. I don't remember anything else. I stayed for about a week in those conditions without having the right to take off my blindfold, my scarf or my veil. I must neither cough nor speak. If I was in urgent need, I was to lift my hand. I was to stay seated the whole time. They didn't even let me lie down. I felt ill! I could have stretched out between those two beds; it was like a coffin. I think it was a small cell, or a room with a bathroom, or perhaps just a bathroom that was used like that. The air was stifling, I was tired. How long were they going to leave my blindfold on? I should certainly be there for some time and when I went elsewhere, they would take my blindfold off. Sometimes the air was so heavy that I felt I was dying, but I woke up after a time and noticed that I was alive! In fact I must have fainted. It was certainly the result of the blows.

I stayed there for a few days, probably a week. One day, they came to fetch me, got me up and made me leave the room. Once outside, I felt that I could breathe and came back to myself. I still don't understand how that week passed. I only have a few memories of it. I barely remember that woman, nothing else. They took me to the entrance of the unit, we went into a big room to the left, where they handed me over to another woman. I was told to take off my blindfold and my veil. When I had done so, I remained in a state of amazement. In front of me was Kiyanoushe, one of those "fighters" who used to take themselves for Che Guevara and who was now dressed in a black veil and a thick scarf. She wanted to search me. She had become exactly like the pasdaran. What a period! The tenacious fighter of a few weeks ago had become a wardress. She tried not to look me in the eyes and gave me so-called advice. She told me a whole heap of ineptitudes.

"The people outside need persons like us, why stay here?" she proffered.

"The people don't need shits like you!" I answered her. *"Don't worry about the people! Do your job!"*

She shut up, and those are the last words I said to her.

She made me go into the unit and I sat down in the same conditions, veiled, my eyes blindfolded, facing the wall between two planks about fifty centimetres apart. A real coffin without a lid. My senses began working properly again. There too, it was cold. I realised that this was Hadji's "machine for making women recant".

The stinkers! They thought they could make us fall for their little game! Those cretins didn't doubt their system for a moment.

Then I remembered Massoud[1]. As if his memory had awaited that moment to come back to me. I remembered his eight years of torture and suffering in prison. His cry, *"What is to be done?"* in Amdjadieh stadium in front of the hundreds of thousands of people who had come to hear him, rang out in my ears. I felt he was at my side.

I remembered the cell and the first interrogation; that night when we counted 120 executions and the one when we enumerated 220 fatal shots. I remembered the executions of Tahmineh and Kobra.

No! It wasn't possible, the God of the Mojahedin said: *"I burden no one beyond his capacities."* Then, it was God himself who had chosen me for this talk, he certainly knows I'm capable of it. So I can do it! I can do it!

It was as if these thoughts had inspired me with a new soul!

---

1. Massoud Rajavi.

A few hours earlier, the pressure of the blindfold was weighing on me like a tombstone. I cried out in my inmost heart: *"But when will they take off this damned blindfold?!"* And now I was preparing myself to live with it.

Hadji, you dirty shit! You will live in frustration because you couldn't conquer a Mojahed. I felt that I had a powerful weapon and shot arrows with all my hatred into the heart and mind of that wild beast. I felt strangely victorious and full of life.

The days passed like this and Hadji came every day, in silence, to check his machine. I felt his infamous presence. It was useless, the machine for making "recanting women" had a serious technical problem. It was no longer a question of mass production. The women who formerly claimed to be "militants" had been the guinea-pigs, but there would be no more of them.

This is how the programme unfolded: getting up between 5 and 6 in the morning, with the call to prayer, three minutes for toilet and ablutions, five minutes for prayer, then we sat in our cage and had breakfast. At noon, three more minutes for toilet, then prayer, the cage and lunch. Then at I don't know what time, three more minutes of toilet and ablutions, then prayer and dinner. Then we stayed seated until midnight. Then, we could at last lie down and sleep, normally for four or five hours, and the next day came. Days, weeks, months went by like that in an interminable manner. Nothing happened and no news came from anywhere.

For praying, there was a sort of screen made of blankets, forming a sort of little room. When I went to pray, I waited for the moment when nobody was watching me to go and have a look outside above the blankets. It was an old-fashioned games room with a pit in the middle. In fact it was the unit's games room. Later I saw one exactly like it in unit 3.

All round the room, by putting boards at every 50 cm, they had made numerous cages, about 80 or 90, and in each one of them, someone was sitting facing the wall. In the pit were the girls' bags and possessions. I tried to recognise the bags to know who was there.

The room was rectangular. When you came in, the bathroom was on the right and the pit on the left; the recanting women were facing the door, in the middle. They had a heater for preparing tea and food. I was five metres from the door and there were five or six other cages before mine. The place for prayer was beyond the door on the left, against a wall running the width of the room, just between two windows. So, when we went to pray, we could take off our blindfolds and see a turret and its warder. I therefore knew exactly how the room was arranged. Every day I checked to see whether a place was empty or whether a new prisoner had been brought in.

Every day, they relayed to us the deafening singing of Ahangaran and other singers, and sprayed us with war propaganda. The loudspeakers poured out news of the regime's total victory at the front of "good over evil". As to the "educational programme", we were fortunately forbidden to go to it, but it was retransmitted to us through loudspeakers so that "we shouldn't lose a crumb of it".

Days and nights in the cage

The transmission of the Qur'an, the call to prayer and the newspaper that I heard every noon through the loudspeakers enabled me to know the date and count the days spent in that section. It was our trump card. The rest of the time, there was silence, nothing but silence and more silence. At first, we didn't notice. In fact I didn't know how effective it was for the torturers. But little by little, I understood that it was a means of torture and constant pressure meant to destroy people's minds. Hadji came and threatened us: *"Think carefully if you want to be reasonable. Here, it's the last judgment!"*

It was terrifying to be cut off from the world. Heavens, what's happened to the other girls? In what state are they? What do they want to do to us? They won't let us out of here, so why don't they execute us? What are my mother and father doing? Where are they searching for me? A throng of thoughts invaded my mind and my soul had too many things to bear. I would have liked to speak to someone, but apart from God and myself, there was no one. So I spoke to God and told him of my sufferings, and then I began to cry. I called to him for help, I asked him to give me the strength to resist and not to let the enemy take hold of me.

I listened attentively to the reading of the Qur'an that was on the radio every day before prayers and reflected on its meaning. I found God's answer there and peace descended into me for a few moments.

But nothing equalled the suffering that the blindfold over my eyes imposed on me. Why didn't they take it off, that damned blindfold? It was the best way of cutting off the individual from outside; it forced him to plunge into himself. Thus they deprived us of the most important sense and the essential means of communicating with the world outside. I told myself that without that blindfold, I could have endured prison for a hundred years. That damned blindfold exasperated me. At the moment of prayer, when I was freed of it for a few minutes and could see the warden's observation turret, I envied the pasdar who was on top because he could see everything.

Even for sleeping, I had to keep it on. The worst was to suffer from insomnia. There had come a time when the flood of thoughts like *"there's no hope that this will ever finish"* prevented me from sleeping in spite of my fatigue. Yet I waited impatiently for the moment when I could lie down and sleep. Whichever way I turned, I still saw that dark, endless tunnel without an opening in front of me. And suddenly dawn came and another day began. Heavens, how could I endure the day, with all this fatigue?

One evening, one of the girls started shouting and saying incoherent things, laughing and crying. The warders took her away; I don't know who she was or what happened to her. It wasn't the first time that a girl lost her head. I came to myself. I realised that by bandaging our eyes and rubbing our nerves raw, Hadji was trying to break us.

I had to sleep at night, otherwise I too would go mad. I was afraid of myself. I was afraid of despair and of not being able to go on. I was afraid of not being able to hold out against the torturers and to end up as a traitor. *"Am I too going to turn into one of those detestable things willing to have everyone else killed so as to stay alive?! No!... My God, no! Hear my prayer, Lord! Have you not said that you never burdened anyone more than she could bear? Don't you see that under this weight my resistance is exhausted? Have you not said that you are even nearer to us than our jugular vein? Have you not said: 'If I am called, I shall answer?' Then, Lord, help me! Help me!"*

When I spoke to Him, I had a feeling of relief. I said to myself: *"Hengameh, God is not a lie, God is not unjust. Perhaps you can do it, that you have the strength. You've put up with it until now! So it's possible, you can do it. You won't be like those trash collaborators. Could you be like them? No! So be strong! Make your mind up! Try to sleep at night? Find the way to do it! The enemy wants to make you powerless so that you'll give in. And even if you did it, do you think they'd leave you in peace? They'd take you down to the lowest depths of betrayal and crime…"*

Then I decided that, when night came, I'd sleep. *"Stop thinking! Think only of sleeping!"* I started counting, beginning with the memory of the trees in our quarter, the windows of our house, going on to those of the dormitory in the university, the number of hospital wards where I had worked since the beginning. I just counted and went on counting, and I don't know when I fell asleep, but the destructive insomnia had ended! This was victory!

The days were very long. To pass the day and make it shorter, I planned it. Especially as they woke us up very early and we had to get up and sit down. We normally began at 5 or 6 in the morning.

Sometimes I tired myself out talking to myself and thinking. I put my head on my knees and fell asleep. But the pasdar woman would hit me on the head, yelling: *"Don't sleep!"* It was forbidden to sleep or even doze for a minute during the day or before midnight. In that state, you were still given blows. The worst was when you were thinking and were suddenly given a violent blow on the head, which struck the wall in front of you. For a few moments, you remained in shock, a prey to giddiness, without understanding where you were or what was going on.

Besides, you had to sit so that your head wasn't above the top of the cage, which was 50 cm high. Otherwise, blows with cables, kicks and punches from the pasdaran soon forced you to bend down. For tall people like me, sitting folded up added to the physical suffering.

At mealtimes, too, no noise must be heard, not even the spoon hitting the plate. If they heard anything, the warders thought we were communicating in Morse code with our neighbours and blows and torture awaited us. We were waiting perpetually for a blow. Danger always seemed imminent. The feeling of insecurity, and fear, plunged us into anguish. In those moments, seconds turned into hours. *"My God, how long can I resist?"*

I had decided to kill myself as soon as I began to lose my mental balance. I had found a way to do it. I should burn myself alive with the lamp which served to heat the meals. It belonged to the pasdaran women, it contained oil and was always alight. I had sworn to myself that before doing it, I would kill those two monsters by crushing their heads against the ground and burning them with me.

Hadji came every day to see if his system was working properly and to try to destroy us even more. *"Nobody will come to your help,"* he used to say sneeringly. *"Your adored Massoud isn't there. Not unless you decide to turn into human beings."* In the torturer's language, all words mean their opposite. *"Deciding"* meant *"lowering your arms"*, *"turning into human beings"* meant *"turning into vultures, into spies, into traitors!"*

Hadji chose a few women from among us, took them outside, beat them black and blue, then asked them to recant. As to those on whom the spies had reported, he persecuted and tortured them right there in the cage. Sometimes, he came noiselessly and covered his victim with punches and kicks. One day, a violent noise rang out. At the same moment, we heard a stifled cry, then the sound of my neighbour's head hitting the wall opposite her. Then we heard Hadji spitting insults: *"You still haven't turned into a human being?!"* he howled. But not a sound came from my neighbour any longer.

One day, I too was his prey. I suddenly felt a weight fall on my head and I thought my neck was sinking into my ribcage. I felt dizzy, my vision was fogged. Then I heard the groans of Hadj Davoud being vituperative. He had surprised me by a blow on the head with his enormous fist.

I realised how cruel the enemy was and how much he hated us. I felt that he wanted to crush me and make me inferior. And this feeling gave me a motive for resisting.

How I could hate them! If I had had a weapon, before killing the torturer Hadj Davoud, I should have killed that Gestapo or another. Those sellers of human beings wrote in their reports to Hadj Davoud that so and so had communicated in Morse with her neighbour by knocking her spoon on her plate. They wrote that, because at mealtimes, with our eyes blindfolded, it happened that spoons did hit plates. They also reported who had coughed, sneezed or made any other noise. You couldn't even cough!

It was very difficult. I couldn't stand it any longer. Ah, that damned blindfold! I felt that my lashes were sinking into my eyes. I wished I had no eyes so as not to feel them any longer. *"Lord, help me! You said that you had given me a burden I could bear! So why am I failing to resist?"*

Sitting had become a problem. I had been sitting down for months now. I hurt everywhere. How could I sit so as to hurt less? Whichever way I turned, it was as if there had been needles on the ground; I felt as if they were sinking into my body. Then I put my hands under me, but they soon grew numb and I had ants in my arms.

I was deep in thought and complaining incessantly, when I suddenly felt someone's presence above my head. *"Hengameh, hello!"* I recognised her stupid voice. It was Sholeh, a recanting woman, a traitor who was in our cell at Evin. She had become one of Hadji's spies and did his dirty work among the cages and coffins.

"Well then! You're still sitting down?!"

"Yes! Does it bother you?" I answered, smiling, freed from all my thoughts.

"She's still laughing!" she exclaimed. *"She's really stubborn!"*

Interesting! So they were waiting till we were no longer willing to sit. Our enemy was watching like a vulture for our corpses. Once more God had helped me by putting me face to face with my enemy. It's a law of resistance: you must neither forget nor ignore your enemy, otherwise you lose your direction. For example, you suffer a thousand pains, your blindfold is a nuisance and you complain. No! you're mistaken, you band of hyenas!

I arranged my blindfold so that, seen from above, it wasn't obvious that it didn't quite cover my eyes. Henceforward I had my eyes and eyelids free and that was enough for me. I had also found a technique for sitting down: my woollen waistcoat! Why hadn't I thought of it sooner? It was soft and thick. During the day, I sat on it and at night it was my pillow. What a good thing my sweet Makhala had sent me! It was as if she had known what it would be used for.

My aunt's name was Mahi. By shortening her first name and adding *"Khaleh"* (*"aunt"* in Persian), we called her Makhala. She was all sweetness. All the time I remained in prison, even if visits were forbidden, she refused to let herself be defeated. She stood outside the prison. Every time, she brought me something, like that grey waistcoat that she had knitted. I thanked her more than once in my heart.

The sound of the dry bread that someone was eating broke the silence. I listened attentively to that sound that came from my right. It was she! Zohreh! Right there beside me. At the time of going to prayer, I saw a corner of her veil. It was her all right. So Zohreh too had been transferred to the cage. Hadji wasn't leaving her alone. So the cry and the impact of the head hitting the wall, was that of hers!

It was Ramadan. I didn't know how much time had passed. I was waiting for Hadji to tire and abandon his machine for turning prisoners into traitors, and look for new methods.

Spring passed and summer came. I had now been there for nearly seven months. Hadji hadn't come for a few days. The traitors' whispers had grown louder and they didn't come around us so much. They seemed bored and showed little eagerness for "working", that is to say torturing us. Sometimes the door opened, much more often than usual, and we heard the breathing of one or more people, as if they were coming and going.

One morning, they called me and took me outside. Against all expectation, they told me I had visitors. After seven months, my poor parents had come. I went to the visiting room. They were there, standing up, behind the glass. A pasdar was beside them, another beside me. Seeing me, my father could not keep back his tears. But my mother, who is a strong woman, managed to control herself. *"Don't cry,"* I told them, *"I don't want to see you unhappy."* My father couldn't speak, he looked at me in tears. I understood that for seven months, they had fought without ceasing and complained to all the regime's social services to obtain this right to visit. Many other parents had struggled in the same way, but still had no news of their children. At one point when the two pasdaran were looking elsewhere, I made the victory sign to my father who still wasn't managing to master himself. Immediately, his eyes began to glow intensely. I laughed. He smiled. *"Don't worry about me,"* I said to him, *"I'm no longer a child and what upsets me is to see you unhappy."* In fact, I wanted them to know that the struggle was going on.

Something must be happening, I thought, on the way back. Otherwise why did they allow visits?

The failure of the machine for making women recant

On the following days, while I was watching the unit from the prayer room, I noticed that the number of bags was decreasing and that some cages were empty. I thought that I might soon be transferred too.

One fine day, I was deep in thought: I was observing, as I did every day, a line of ants which were running along the wall. I watched their activities and their movements from under my blindfold. I had made their acquaintance seven months earlier. I may say that we had become friends. I knew their habits. Above all, they were strangely fond of flies. When they found one, the news spread like lightning and they attacked the dead or dying fly together. Without giving it the slightest rest, they first of all pulled off its head which they took into the anthill, then they cut off its legs and then the huge body. As to the wings, they tore them from the body and put them in a place some distance from the entrance to the anthill. There was a mountain of flies' wings. I still don't know why. Perhaps a fly's wing is tasteless or else too hard or ... I was thinking about it when I felt a breath above my head, then I heard the voice of someone unknown saying hello to me.

"*Who are you?*" I asked.

"*Why don't you answer my greetings?*"

I understood that it was a pasdar or a mullah. In short, it was a new agent. But I wanted to know who it was. Besides, I didn't care a curse from now on whether I was behaving calmly or not. I was ready to take the consequences of my attitude.

"*We have come to inspect your situation.*"

"*I haven't asked for anything.*"

He understood that he wasn't welcome and that I didn't want to speak to him.

"*My sister, don't blame Islam for acts of this kind!*"

"*You can be sure that we're not blaming Islam for it, or we shouldn't be here.*"

I think he didn't understand what I meant to say.

"*I have come to inspect your living conditions. People have made complaints to Mr. Montazeri[2], so I came to hear what you had to say. In what situation do you find yourself?*"

His ridiculous question made me laugh.

---

2. The Ayatollah Hossein Ali Montazeri, at that time Khomeini's heir.

"Sir, I am blindfolded, but yours are open. Just look around you. Why are you asking me this question? If it doesn't bother you, go away! I have nothing to say to you. I'm well. Goodbye!" And I lowered my head.

"Goodbye, my sister," he replied.

I had learned what I wanted to learn and I didn't want to speak to that mullah any more. Little by little, the warders emptied all the cages. One day, they finally grouped us all together and transferred us to a room in unit 3. We had called it "the isolation room". We could see that there too had been a system of Hadji's cages. They had gathered up the boards. But the prayer place formed of blankets was still in position. And that sign was enough for me.

Return in triumph

When you came in at the door, there was a little corridor, with lavatories on the left. Then you entered the room. It was quite vast and rectangular. There was a rather large window on the right-hand wall, looking onto a garden.

I went in, and I no longer wore a blindfold! All the girls were there. I gave a quick glance at them to see if there were any I knew. Azam and some other girls from unit 7 were sitting in a corner. I ran joyfully towards them and asked them for news of the others. I couldn't keep still. Azam, who was sitting down, said to me calmly: *"Hengameh, sit down for a minute and wait to see what happens!"* I realised that I was making too much noise and that we still didn't have enough perspective on our situation. I calmed myself a little. Something wasn't right. The silence was particularly heavy.

Some girls who had come back from the "habitable units" had become mentally ill. In the isolation room, I learned that Shekar had also been in the "habitable units". I don't know what people went through there so as to make everyone come back so upset.

Parvine had taken shelter in the prayer place and wouldn't come out of it; she insulted everyone from there. Roxana, a young girl, walked about weeping and talking to herself. She kept repeating: *"I'm a dog! I'm a donkey!"* Farideh cursed herself, wept and sat facing the wall for hours. Mansoureh was there too. I went towards her and called her. She turned sharply towards me and sat down. She held out her arm to tell me not to come nearer. She shook her head and backed away while still sitting down.

"Mansoureh, it's me, Hengameh!"

But she went still farther away, in tears. I stopped going forward.

Heavens, what had happened to them? Why did they all seem to have lost their reason? They had come back from a mysterious place, the "habitable units".

The warders opened the door. They made a thin girl come into the isolation room, wearing a dark blue coat and a scarf. Then they left. She stopped in the middle of the room, her face stiff, looking straight in front. She was pressing a small Qur'an to her heart. *"Farzaneh!"* an astonished and horrified girl called her. *"But what have they done to you?"*

I don't know who had told me that she had been in a position of responsibility, had managed to gain Hadji's trust and had escaped from the prison. But she had been re-arrested and tortured. And now, they had brought her back to us, cracked, stiff and silent. She absolutely never spoke. She stayed in one position, standing or sitting, sometimes for seventeen hours at a stretch! It was astonishing, she didn't eat, didn't go to the lavatories. Seeing her, you felt your heart crushed with grief. Nobody knew what they had done to her, because she could no longer say anything about it.

Of the girls from unit 7, there were Sepideh, Maryam, Parvine, Azam and Zohreh Chavoshi. They called Zohreh again; Hadji was still putting pressure to recant so that he could free her. Zohreh's family belonged to Hezbollah and insisted on trying to recover her. Zohreh hadn't been arrested on political ground and the regime had no reason to keep her in prison.

Hadji's problem was that he couldn't tell Hezbollahis that a girl who hadn't been a supporter of the Mojahedin when she was arrested had become one in prison while under torture. That's why he was using all his strength to make Zohreh crack. Without success.

"When we were in the cage," said Zohreh, *"Hadji took me outside. He told me I must recant or else he'd hit me till I died of it. I answered that he wanted me to spy and I wouldn't do it. I wouldn't even give him out-of-date information. I wouldn't write a word to him either. He could do what he liked with me. And as Hadji didn't know what to do, he thrashed me. I cried out under the avalanche. I shouted at him: 'If you're a man, take off this blindfold and free my hands, and we'll see who hits whom, you dirty coward!'"*

Hadji really did find himself in a cleft stick. Finally, they freed Zohreh who never cracked in the isolation room. I saw her much later outside the prison. After her liberation, she wanted to join the Mojahedin in Iraq. She disappeared without a trace. She must have been arrested and killed by the regime.

Among the Marxists, only four had resisted the cages and come to the isolation room. They said that there were no Marxists in the other units either and that they had all recanted. One of the four was called Shahnaz. She was a schoolgirl. *"Just lately,"* she said, *"Hadji didn't know what to do any longer. He even came to say to all four of us: 'Just pretend to pray and I'll take you to the unit.' But we didn't accept."* They were struggling, honourable women who were responsible for their words and deeds, and paid the price for it.

Part Six

The "habitable units"

The mentally ill

Difficult days were to come, as the mentally ill women made things much harder. A new torture had started in the isolation room, a psychological torture.

Farideh walked about and insulted everyone. She cursed herself and sometimes hit herself. It was the result of the "habitable units". The warders tortured the prisoner, then set up a scenario to make her believe that another one had denounced her. They went on torturing her by repeating that so and so had said that, until she was convinced that she had been betrayed.

They also asked her to write or speak about the others and continued the torment until they got something. Then they used the girl, or her so-called confessions, to put pressure on the others. Finally, they put the people in question face to face, thus creating a climate of distrust and hate between the prisoners. It was for this reason that some of them were even afraid to look at one another. Sometimes they victimised a prisoner simply to make her say whether a girl had looked at her or not, said hello to her or not. That was also why the prisoners spent hours facing the wall: so as not to see anyone and not to be tortured. It was Shekar who told me that afterwards.

Henceforward, Farideh insulted everyone and had undermined the morale of all the girls. One day she said something about Massoud (Rajavi). This was new, she'd never done it before. Immediately Shahin Jolghazi stood up, caught her by the neck and shook her. Farideh stopped speaking. She took her face between her hands and said to her: *"Listen to me carefully. Be mad, be at the end of your tether, be what you like, you can even curse yourself. But if you pronounce Massoud's name once more, I'll kill you! Understood?!"* She nodded. Shahin let her go and sat down again.

A few hours later, they took Shahin away and savagely tortured her. I got to know Shahin Jolghazi in the isolation room. She roared like a lioness and was extremely serious-minded. She had spent months in the cage. I think she came from unit 8. She was executed at the time of the massacre of political prisoners in 1988. Throughout all those years, she never stopped being tortured in the disciplinary units of Evin. After Shahin made this clear, Farideh said nothing more about Massoud.

Shouranguiz Karimi was also in the isolation room. At first, I didn't recognise her. I knew her before being in prison, at a time when she was still very young. Three years later, you would have said she was thirty years older. She looked like a little old woman, her eyes hollow and her back curved. She had one arm paralysed and could no longer lift it. One day, Hadji came to the isolation room to pour out his usual imbecilities. When he asked, "Where's the doctor, Madame Shouri?" I realised that this old woman was actually Shouranguiz, the medical student, who had once come to our home.

When he had left, I went to see her.

"*Shouranguiz, it's really you?*"

"*Yes.*"

"*So why didn't you say so?*"

She smiled. Normally, the people who were the subject of particular investigation tried not to grow too close to the others for fear of making trouble for them. Sometimes, even, when other prisoners wanted to come near them, they discouraged them, saying: "*They want to execute me. It's better for you not to be seen with me in public.*" Shouranguiz had endured terrible tortures. When her torturers had hung her up by the arms, she had dislocated her shoulder and it had never since then gone back to its proper place. In spite of her condition, she took part in all the daily tasks that were shared out among the girls. She took care of the unit and wouldn't let anyone work instead of her. She did everything with one hand. She was particularly calm, and showed remarkable coolness. Hadji was watching her, because in spite of all his tortures, Shouranguiz resisted with the same courage and firmness. She never came back to the ordinary units, she remained in the disciplinary ones. They finally executed her too, in the 1988 massacre.

One day, a certain mullah Ansari came to the isolation room. "*We come from Mr. Montazeri to inspect the situation in the prisons. There have been complaints about how things have been done without permission and the imam hasn't been told about it...*" He lied as easily as he spoke. Khomeini, that butcher, confirmed executions himself. He had given a free hand to all his torturers, emphasising that "*the life, the property and the honour of the Mojahedin belonged [to them].*" And now, that demagogic mullah wanted to mock us. He thought he was dealing with a band of ignorant

Hezbollahis. *"You to are the children of Muslims,"* he went on. *"We want to set you free. We only want you not to take up arms against us. Otherwise, don't people insult the imam? Yet nobody's doing anything to them. You're only being asked to lay down your arms!"*

"Excuse me, sir! Which of us had any arms to lay down?" said one girl.

"Yes, we know many of you haven't committed that kind of crime. That's just what we're investigating."

And he went on with his speech. We understood then that the factions in the regime were having an impact on the prisons. Especially as all their stupid efforts had led to nothing. After this period when visits were forbidden, after the problem had been publicised thanks to protests and pressure from families, it was then their turn to split apart on the subject.

One day, they called Maryam Mohammadi Bahman-Abadi. When she came back, she was very happy. In her joy, she took the girls in her arms and twirled them around.

"But what's going on?"

"I've been awarded a reduction in my sentence!"

"Wonderful! That means you're being set free?"

"No, but from a lifer, I've gone down to fifteen years."

"Well, that's not a reason for being happy!" we said, disappointed.

"You really think I'm naïve enough to think they'd set me free? And that I should be pleased about that! No, come on! On the other hand, just think about Gestapo and those other shits who are just waiting for us to give in. They'll put on such faces!"

Maryam too was executed in the 1988 massacre.

After two months in the isolation room, at the end of the summer of 1984, they finally sent me back into a group of ten people in unit 7. I no longer remember what time of day it was. I was very impatient to see my friends. Gestapo and Tavous, her colleague, were standing up. You should have seen Gestapo's face! I wished she could have been right opposite me so that I could throw her a punch. But she seemed to have understood that she mustn't stay in front of us. We went into the unit and the girls sprang on us. There were fewer of them. Ategheh, Maryam and little Atiyeh were no longer there. It was said that they had been transferred to Babol. Taking us in their arms, the girls told us that many had been taken to the disciplinary unit number 8 and to various other units.

Zahra came up and took me in her arms. She was crying.

"*Why are you crying?*"

"*But what have they done to you to make you look like that?*"

I looked at myself in the mirror. Not having seen the sun for nine months, I had grown quite white. We had grown much thinner too. I had one strand of hair that had turned white, I don't know when, and the girls said that I looked like Indira Gandhi. We hugged each other and joked, full of joy.

One of the girls from Sari came to tell me: "*Gestapo and her troop kept on coming to tell us: 'You will soon see your friends from the resistance in an interview.' They spread a rumour that you had given in and they tried to frighten us. But we knew that you wouldn't give in and that you wouldn't betray.*"

The recanting women and the spies no longer looked proud. They were ill at ease. It was the result of the problems and divisions in the prison's administration, and the consequence of speeches like those of the mullah Ansari. For the moment everything was against those recant-ing women and nobody defended them. The regime had thrown all the blame on them so as to protect its agents. Above all, the recanting women were frightened of the prisoners, because they knew how many people they had caused to be executed.

This fear had taken hold above all of the torturers and executioners, to the point that Hadj Davoud and Lajevardi lived in the prison and didn't go outside any longer. Hadj Davoud had even installed his wife and children there.

Even face to face with the Mojahedin who were to be executed, the torturers didn't show themselves without masks. If they were frightened, one can imagine what a state of mind the recanting women were in.

In unit 7, I suddenly noticed Mother Massoumeh. It was her all right, Massoumeh Ilekhani in person. She looked a great deal thinner and older. I took her in my arms and tried spontaneously to catch her long braided hair. But there was only one fine, short strand left.

"Where's your hair gone?"

"Let it go!" she said, looking at me kindly. *"What use is hair to me when we've lost the best people among us?"*

She seemed so sad! We didn't have time to argue. Night had fallen and I went on chatting with the girls. Gestapo was watching us. I was sitting down, talking to Jamileh, when Tavous, the piece of garbage who had sent the girls to the "cages", the "coffins" and the "habitable units", came to sit down shamelessly beside us. I knew that Gestapo had sent her to spy on us.

"Greetings, Hengameh! How are you?"

"Who asked you to come and talk to me? Clear off!"

She scuttled away like a rat.

"Why did you say that to her? Tomorrow they'll take you to unit 8," said Jamileh.

"So I should hope, because Shekar's there too."

In fact, I was no longer making calculations and didn't care … What more could they do to me than they had done already?

Next day, during our walk, I went to see Mother Massoumeh. We started to chat and she showed me photos she had been sent, including one of her son who had grown.

"It's his photo a few days before his death …"

"Before his what, mother?!"

"Don't be sad! They've killed so many children from the best of us: Kobra, Fati, Afsaneh, Nahid and the others …. My son's one of them as well. His blood's no redder than that of the others. He too was killed, in practice, by Khomeini."

And she told me how, while he was playing on the balcony, he tipped over into space and was killed at once. Not wanting to make me sadder, she changed the subject and showed me another photo. How wise and patient she was!

There was a girl whom I did not know, sitting beside us, on the steps of the exercise yard. She was tall, with a long face.

"You're called Hengameh?" she asked me.

"Yes!"

"You were a nurse?"

"Yes! How do you know me?"

"By your way of speaking, your gestures. Shekar spoke to me a lot about you. You're exactly as she described you. I'm called Mina."

"You were with Shekar!" I exclaimed, happily. *"Where? When? How?"*

"Not now!" she said calmly.

"No, please!"

"Listen, I'm not in a good situation, they're watching me closely. You'd better not talk too much."

"That doesn't matter, please tell me about Shekar."

Mother Massoumeh interjected:

"But you don't realise, don't talk, listen! You're still just as imprudent as always!"

I had to stop. Mina was one of the rare girls who had come back from the "habitable units" without losing her reason. But she was silent and prudent.

I saw Mother Massoumeh for the last time in that same unit. Afterwards, I heard that she had gone mad in prison. On her last visit she had been told of the death of her elder son. Strange fate! Her uncle had taken him into the mountains for hiking and he had had a fatal fall. So both her sons had been killed, one after the other. When that news hit her, she plunged into a silence that she never broke. She stayed for two more years in prison, a prey to serious depression and a deep mental unbalance. She was only set free when they were sure that having tipped into madness, she would never recover her health or have a normal life.

Such a strong woman: even the Shah's tortures and prison hadn't been able to shake her. Then she had passed four years in Khomeini's gaols.

Mother Massoumeh was never tried, no verdict was ever given against her. Throughout her imprisonment, she kept an indeterminate status. The regime had nothing against her. Even with its lopsided laws, it hadn't managed to set up a dossier against her.

Khomeini's prisons really were like no others. One could perhaps compare them to the Nazis' death camps. But in the camps, only the human being was killed. In the mullahs' prisons, if someone hadn't died under torture, if she had survived the "cage", the "coffin", the "habitable units", and the suffering that transcends understanding, if she had escaped without going mad, she ended up being snatched by death during the political prisoners' massacre of 1988 that took place after years of torture.

I think one must have lived through it to understand it. No one can describe it, simply because the words to do so do not exist.

I find Shekar again

Night fell. What we were expecting had happened. They called our team of ten girls. They made us leave the unit and made us stand in a row behind the entrance.

"Who's Hengameh?" asked a pasdar woman new to the unit, wanting to check if I was present.

"That's me!"

"For having failed to respect the unit's rules, you are all transferred to unit 8."

I nearly shouted for joy: *"Lord! I'm going to see Shekar!"* but I choked it back. We went to unit 8. The line walked on, but I wanted to run. When we arrived, the unit exploded with joy. Most of the girls from 7 were there.

I had my shoes in my hand and I kept catching my feet in my veil which had fallen. The girls were arriving from all sides, taking us in their arms and covering us with kisses. But I was looking for Shekar. We were stuck in one place because there were so many people at the entrance. Suddenly, right at the end of the flock, on the left, in front of cell 4, I saw her. Shekar! She was standing on tiptoe, signalling to me with her hand and shouting my name. There was so much noise that I couldn't hear her. Her face was bathed in tears.

"*Shekar!*" I shouted, letting fall everything I had in my hands and trying to clear a path to her. Shekar too plunged into the crowd to reach me. Heavens! I had been waiting for this moment for three years. We threw ourselves into each others' arms. She had laid her head on my shoulder, endlessly repeating my name. She was shouting, she was crying. She sank her face into my neck, repeating: "*Hengameh! Hengameh! You were my only friend! You were my only friend!*" Suddenly, she turned towards the girls, shouting: "*She's my only friend! My only friend!*"

That surprised me. And then I realised what was happening all around us: the girls were surrounding us and crying silently. If I heard Shekar so clearly, it was because of this silence. She went on clinging to me and crying. I took her by the shoulders with one arm; she had seized my other arm in both hands and was holding it tightly. I led her towards that cell where she was and towards the nearest wall. The girls opened a path for us and scattered. Nobody came up to us. We sat down, hand in hand.

"*Are you well?*" I asked her. I was looking at her, she seemed sad and tired. She was much thinner. She had a pony tail. She was still just as tidy and well-groomed. I put my hand in her hair and messed it up. That same hair which I was used to styling, then messing up so as to annoy her. "*So, are you well?*" She smiled, her eyes full of tears, anxiously, and made a movement with her head. A girl passed in front of us, smiling. Shekar's eyes followed her. Without taking her eyes away from her, she whispered to me: *"Hengameh, don't trust them! Don't trust anyone!"* And then, in a sad, distressed voice, as if she had remembered something, as if she wanted to justify herself, she added: *"They wanted to bring my mother here, imagine, my poor mother, here! Heavens!"* and her tears began to flow again. I stroked her face.

"Shekar, what's happened? What have they done to you? Who wanted to bring your mother here?"

"They did!"

I realised that she wasn't in a normal state, that she was a prey to deep anguish, sorrow and anxiety.

I changed the subject. I spoke to her of our former friends, of the amusing memories that we shared, of sandwiches on the eve of examinations, of the tea we made in secret in the dormitory, of Mrs. Guilak, of Mrs. Khosravi and other teachers we bullied. I reminded her of the day when I was trapped in the fruit-tree and when she and Soussan ran away with the fruit, leaving me alone up there. At the time, we used to laugh madly together. But today Shekar did nothing but laugh. I was astonished by the behaviour of the other girls who didn't come near us.

A further experience of the monsters

I stood up to tidy my things.

"I'm coming back so that we can eat together. You bring what you've got, too! I've nothing for the moment."

When I left, Jila, whom I didn't know, called me into a corner. She had been in the same unit as Shekar. She was crying.

"You know what? We thought Shekar would never get over it, that she'd never again be able to laugh, greet anyone, talk. Today, she's alive again. The little nurse from our unit's alive again, as she was before. Ever since the "habitable unit", she's done nothing but cry. She stays sitting down for hours facing the wall and doesn't speak to anyone. And those dirty recanting women don't let her go and you can't even get near her. She didn't speak to us, she was in anguish. She didn't speak to the recanting women who were all round her either. She was afraid of everything. Because they're watching for the moment when she'll crack. And you can see that they're pushing her to the limit so as to finish her off."

The hyenas! Those same hyenas, whom I knew, were waiting to throw themselves on Shekar's corpse! I couldn't believe that my Shekar had become like the other girls in the "habitable units". But it was true. She too had lost her reason. Fortunately, the torturers hadn't yet been able to turn her into a zombie and, in spite of all the tortures, she hadn't forgotten Massoud and the Mojahedin. That was her lifebuoy.

Afterwards, I wanted to check what were her relations with the traitors and the recanting women who clung to her skirts and, taking account of her difficulties, up to what point she had advanced towards them.

"What did you say to those women who were all round you? It's important to me."

"Hengameh!" she said, looking offended. *"You think I betrayed?"*

After a short silence, she went on, as if she felt obligated to answer.

"They wanted to force me to recant. I was really in a very bad way, but I knew who they were and what they wanted.

I knew why they had started being so nice to me. But I didn't speak to them. I've never betrayed. I shall never betray! Do you believe me, tell me?!"

"Of course, I believe you."

When she was sure of it, she turned her eyes away and went on speaking.

When I went back to her, it was time for dinner.

"Hengameh, they told us that we mustn't eat together, nobody has the right to eat with someone else. They said all we could do was invite each other to start eating!"

"Who told you that stupid thing? Hadji? Because he said something as imbecile as that, we'll respect it to the letter. There! Now, you can invite me to start eating."

"Please, dear friend."

"Thank you, dearest."

And we started swallowing the watery yoghurt that they had given us for supper. And we laughed at Hadji, at all the torturers and all the recanting women. The yoghurt seemed delicious to us that evening.

"Hengameh, you look like Indira Gandhi."

"The girls say that too. That's good. At least we're like important people in some way."

And we burst out laughing.

"Don't wear your hair in a bun, let it hang down," said Shekar.

"No, it's better like that."

"No! Otherwise they'll say you're politically active."

"Well, let them. It's true, isn't it?"

"No! Then it'll start, they'll take you away, they'll hurt you," she insisted, very anxiously.

I understood that such things had been excused for torture in the *"habitable units,"* which had driven those prisoners half mad.

"Shekar, forget the habitable unit! You're here now, it's over, don't think about it."

I hoped that if she avoided thinking about it she'd find her mental balance again, for every memory disturbed her profoundly. Whatever I wanted to say or do, I first had to erase and destroy what her torturers had engraved in her mind. But, thank God, it wasn't too difficult, because Shekar listened to me.

The "habitable unit" remained an enigma for me, a frightful and strange enigma. From what I had heard here and there from the girls, I had more or less understood that in there, whatever you did or didn't do ended with torture in any case. If they talked, for example, they were accused of having talked, and if they said nothing, they were accused of being silent. No matter whether they had done anything or not. Everything was a pretext for torture, on the spot and under the eyes of the others. It was for this reason that the prisoners in the "habitable units" forbade one another to do the most ordinary things, such as saying hello or looking at someone. They stayed for hours and days on end facing the wall, sitting down, motionless and silent.

Shekar ate very little, and when she swallowed something, she turned away immediately to vomit in a little box. She had a gastric ulcer. She had had several haemorrhages, but that vomiting was nervous. She no longer wanted to feed herself.

"I throw up everything I eat."

"That's not serious. Eat! It doesn't matter if you throw it up afterward.s It's better than not eating."

She agreed and the strangest thing is that her vomiting lessened after a few days.

A slap for the traitor doctor

Massoumeh Joushaghani was also in our unit. She had been a senior nurse in the infectious ward at the Thousand-Bed Hospital. Before being sacked, Shekar had worked with her. I had seen her when I had visited Shekar in the Thousand-Beds. Massoumeh's husband taught at the university where he was an active member of the opposition. After the resistance burst out on 20 June 1981, being unable to arrest him, the regime had arrested Massoumeh in his stead. In spite of all their tortures, the pasdaran hadn't got anything out of her that would have enabled them to arrest her husband, and she had been condemned to three years in prison. Massoumeh hadn't taken part in any activities with the Mojahedin, but she defended the girls in prison, and that was why Hadj Davoud hated her. In compensation, the girls adored her.

When she arrived in unit 7, we became friends. We had in common the Mojahedin, Shekar and our profession. Massoumeh profoundly hated the recanting women and the traitors. She had learned what they were like and she had traced a very precise line of demarcation between them. As she was a nurse, the warders had taken her to work in the infirmary. She had gone there with the consent of all the girls.

She worked there with Dr. Hosseini, a former member of the Peykar[1] political group who had recanted and frankly collaborated with Hadj Davoud. When one has be-

1. A Marxist group which has since disappeared from the political scene.

trayed one's people, it's ridiculous to speak of professional ethics. That doctor hadn't the slightest respect for his profession. In the conditions of that prison, there were doctors whose views differed from those of the Mojahedin but who kept their distance from the torturers. They cared for the wounded and ill in a professional and humane way, and sometimes opposed the pasdaran, even if they had to pay the price for it afterwards.

But that Dr. Hosseini, who knew that the girls in unit 8 were the most resistant, didn't care for them. This abandonment made them a prey to additional suffering in the infirmary's beds. One day, revolted by that traitor's indifference, Massoumeh grew angry and roundly criticised him. As Hadj Davoud was present, Dr. Hosseini wanted to build himself up.

"But what's happening to you? They're not your cousins, so why worry about them so much?"

Then Massoumeh, in front of Hadj Davoud, gave him a slap fit to knock his head off.

"No, you dirty bought creature, the traitors are your cousins!" And she gave him a sound correction.

After this adventure, Massoumeh was transferred to unit 8 to be punished. Henceforward all three of us were in it together. Massoumeh too was delighted to see that Shekar was getting better.

You have made a child's toy of me...

Mullah Ansari came several times to unit 8 to try to rub out the past. *"People have a bad image of unit 8,"* he said one day. *"It's a unit like the others. To erase this image, we'll declare it's a 'normal' unit."* And the warders came to open a door onto the exercise yard.

As if one could forget the crimes that Hadji and his pasdaran had commited in that unit; as if it was possible to erase the jammed, closed cells and the tortures inflicted on the girls.

At the time of these events, Hadj Davoud and his torturers vanished; others replaced them. Lajevardi too changed his job.

During this short period of transfers, prisoners were released. The few prisoners who did get out alive, were set free at that moment.

Shekar's health improved little by little, coming almost back to normal. But she still remained sad and depressed. When she described the *"habitable units,"* she said: *"The cages where you were, were resting places for us: sitting facing the wall and waiting for night to fall and day to dawn."* She was on fire with hysteria when she spoke of the traitors: *"It's because of them that they crushed Fatemeh, otherwise she'd never have given in!"*

It would seem that the torturers raped Fatemeh under the others' eyes. I didn't understand Shekar when she spoke of "crushing" and "breaking". Did it mean that? When Shekar reached that stage, she began trembling and couldn't go on speaking.

"They lived with us in the same place," she said of the pasdaran. *"You can't imagine, you can't know what it means, when I tell you that those animals lived with us...*

"We were in Gohardasht prison. One day they took 40 girls and brought them here. They were repulsive. They said they wanted to do a scientific experiment and that we were the guinea-pigs. We knew they were going to make us suffer, but we didn't know how. They forced us to stay on our feet all

day, without water or food. I was able to count up to six days. Then I don't remember what happened. After a very long time, we lost consciousness and fell to the ground. But they revived us with blows and forced us to go on standing. Sometimes, however hard they hit, the girl didn't regain consciousness. Then they abandoned her until she came to herself and started again, over and over.

"We didn't know what they wanted to do, until the day when they took us to the 'habitable unit'. We were blindfolded all the time. That's where the tortures started. They told us 'You're dogs!' or "You're donkeys!' and forced us to repeat it. When under torture you said 'I'm a donkey' the torturer said to us: 'Now you're a donkey, you must bray!' and then 'You must carry us', and they sat on us so that we should carry them. Then they said: 'Write a thousand times: I am a donkey,' then they went on: 'Now write it two thousand times,' and it went on and on."

And then, as if she had lost everything, as if her whole dignity had been humiliated and crushed, Shekar collapsed. I then remembered that in the isolation room, Roxana used to walk to and fro, like a sleepwalker, repeating incessantly, in tears: *"I'm a dog! I'm a donkey!"* At the time I didn't manage to understand the reason for that behaviour.

Sometimes when Shekar was describing the "habitable unit" it was I who couldn't listen any longer, it was I who lost my reason. Lord! But what did they do to human beings? Who will ever be able to believe it? Lord! Where are you? Where are you?

As if in those moments, one could find no release except God. It is only he who can bear those moments; the heart and brain of a human being would have exploded.

I remembered that sometimes, when Shekar was deep in thought, she murmured a poem. She wasn't interested in poetry, so I asked myself what poem it was that she repeated so often.

"I was a noble religious woman
"You have made a child's toy of me."

Before prison, Shekar was a very serious-minded girl, respected and loved. She was always elegant and well-dressed: she had, as they say, class. I never saw her behave carelessly.

Khomeini's cannibals had forced her to do things that had crushed her, like other girls ...

I had been with Shekar for two weeks now. Her condition had grown very much better. Not only did one no longer see any sign of mental unbalance, but she had become as she was before, a fighting Mojahed on top of her form. We imagined plans for changing places with each other during visits. We had both asked our parents to come simultaneously and ask for a visit, so that I could see her father and mother, and she could see mine. *"Shekar, get ready for my father to call you by all those funny names we used to have."* And she burst out laughing.

"How I miss your mother!" she used to say; *"I'd love to see her again."* Our deep friendship had drawn our families very close together. At every visit, my mother began by asking for news of her and her mother asked anxiously after me.

My farewell to Shekar

It was night. We were sitting with Shekar and Massoumeh, arguing.

"I'm sure you and Massoumeh will be set free, but I'll stay here," said Shekar.

"But who said you would stay?" I protested.

"They won't set me free," she flung at me, looking me straight in the eyes.

Suddenly, Sharareh came in with her black veil and her scarf. She had been part of the resistance for a week, but at present she had recanted. As soon as she saw me she turned pale and turned her eyes away. *"You remember?"* I asked her; but she didn't answer. She simply announced: *"Let Shekar Mohammad-Zadeh come with all her things."*

She came from unit 3 which was known for its re-canting women. In fact, there were only a few recanting women, but as these were mostly transferred to unit 3, it had acquired that bad reputation. But perhaps that was another lie on the part of the regime, who wanted to make people believe that they had managed to turn a whole unit around. I suddenly saw Shekar stop dead, repeating: *"I won't go! I won't go!"*

The recanting women had been at their dirty work again. They had reported that Shekar had gone back to be-ing a "hypocrite" and "bad". In fact, those traitors meant that she hadn't become a corpse for those hyenas. They were making a mistake in thinking they could make Shekar and all the other Shekars into corpses. Shekar had reached a peak in her convictions at which even the absence of psy-chological balance hadn't been able to make her a traitor. She had left them with that frustration for ever. I knew that henceforward they could never rob her of her humanity.

Even if separating myself from Shekar and being far away from her was as bitter to me as poison, I had per-suaded her to leave without causing problems, so that they shouldn't take her away by force. When Shekar went out through the unit's door, I stayed quite still, looking at her fixedly. I called on all my strength so as not to cry. But her face was turned towards me, flooded with tears. I wanted to engrave her image and her presence forever on my soul. An evil foreboding told me that I should never see her again. My heart implored the Lord: *"Shekar! Shekar!"* and I struggled to hold back my sobs. They were there under my eyelids, forcing themselves out, ready to flow. At the last moment, Shekar turned round and gave me a last look, and from far off, she stretched out a supplicating hand towards me. I too stretched out my hand through those horrible bars that my heart had crossed. When she had passed through the unit's iron door, my hand was still stretched out towards her and all my soul was crying out: *"Shekar!"*

I don't know who was beside me, but she came to comfort me. *"Tell them, tell them that nobody must come and see me, I need to be alone, I beg you!"* and I went to take shelter in a little bit of solitude on the bed at the top of the cell, and under the covers I shed all the tears that I had held back until then.

For three days running I had fever and pains. I dreamed of Shekar, my sweet one, my gentle one, my friend; a friendship which I never found again.

The girls told me later about Shekar's trajectory until 1988. She always gave proof of her fidelity to the values she had chosen to defend. Before giving her life during the massacre of political prisoners, she went through the individual cells, the disciplinary units, unit 311, then to what was called the "rest" unit. She suffered a great deal with perpetual torture sessions and illnesses. She had become weak and crumpled over. It was hard to recognise her. But the girls who had been with her never stopped saying: *"She has a spirit as strong as a mountain, firm and unshakeable; nothing can make her bend."* It was because she had joined her soul to the resistance of a whole people, that she had forged a weapon capable of bringing her torturers to their knees. No torture could get the better of her.

My liberation

A few days after the end of my sentence, I was called. It was mullah Nasseri.

"You've undergone your punishment. Are you ready to give an interview on television?"

"No!"

And I went back to the unit. I didn't think I should be set free. And a little later, I was transferred to Evin.

I asked myself what was happening. It was perhaps for a new series of interrogations and tortures. But after two days I was released. Makhala and my father came to fetch me. It was about twenty days after they had been told of my liberation, and they came every day to the outside of the prison. That's how they got me back.

As we left, I asked them to stop. I wanted to see Evin for the last time. I looked at Khomeini's Beast crouching in the valley.

How many hearts are still beating behind those walls! How many eyes are looking at the sky and the sunrise behind those little barred windows! *"Be damned! O' you monster! Be damned!"* howled my heart. *"How many dear people have you devoured? How many hopes have you reduced to ashes? Be damned, you who have stolen our loved ones. Be damned for eternity!"*

I remembered little Rouzbeh and his great dream, and I screamed to the face of the Beast: *"I swear by God that we will demolish you, we will destroy you!"*

And I set out...

Table of contents